Praise for Light Up

Light Up is a must read for both new and experienced coaches, showing you how to use the transformative power of metaphors. Lyssa translates theoretical insights into effective coaching practices to leverage the power of metaphors in fostering meaningful client transformations. With multiple coaching demonstrations and significant examples, this book will help you create many lightbulb moments in your coaching conversations.

Dr. Marcia Reynolds, MCC, author of *Coach the Person, Not the Problem* and *Breakthrough Coaching*

When you learn to work with metaphors with your clients, you help them explore new and sacred caverns, you give them wings, and you get that much closer to unlocking their greatness. This book shows you how to become more skillful with your language and a more powerful coach as a result.

Michael Bungay Stanier, author of *The Coaching Habit* and *How to Work with (Almost) Anyone*

"Remarkable" barely scratches the surface. "Tour de Force" would be better. Lyssa has created a rich tapestry of the science of coaching with metaphor. Her dedicated studies of psychological theories and their contribution to coaching is long overdue and expertly woven. I have long been acknowledged for my own use of metaphor in my work as a coach, a coach educator, and now, as a coach supervisor. After reading Lyssa's masterpiece, I feel like a beginner. What a wonderful place to be as a senior practitioner!

Samuel P Magill Sr. MCC, Pioneer of Coaching Supervision in North America

Lyssa's book *Light Up: The Science of Coaching with Metaphors* is a treasure trove of evidence-based ideas and concepts to enrich your practice. It is a book that you will want to re-read again and again. Each time you dip in, you will find another gem that you can use in your setting, whether as a coach, mentor supervisor, or coach educator.

Dr. Elizabeth Crosse, MCC, Mentor Coach, Supervisor, and Research Practitioner

Lyssa has crafted a masterwork in both her distinctive certification program and its accompanying book, *Light Up*. This book delves into the neuroscience of how metaphors work in the brain and then seamlessly weaves them with wisdom and integrates them into the foundational competencies of professional coaching. Lyssa's insights will inspire everyone in the coaching arena, empowering them to create deep conversations with both clients and fellow coaches. Her pioneering efforts in this arena are truly commendable.

Otto Siegel, MCC, Co-author of *Yes, You Are a Genius*

Metaphors provide a process of combining different ideas into a coherent gestalt to stimulate new perceptions and understanding. Learning to listen to the client's metaphors reveals the coach's use of listening, presence, and creativity. *Light Up, The Science of Coaching with Metaphors* is a guide, a resource, and a tool for all coaches who wish to integrate and/or strengthen their use of metaphors for their client's enhancement, reflection, and learning. Lyssa articulates a new way of thinking about listening for metaphors. There is important neuroscience on how the brain responds to metaphors. And, as Lyssa says, "while clients may use metaphors unconsciously, they do not use them unintentionally." Using the clients' metaphors is pivotal. The client's mind has connected meaning, and the coach can leverage that to provoke awareness and new perspectives. As a coach, this book will assist you in deeper listening and partnership. As a client, being heard and using your metaphors to explore your experience is the transformative moment that opens unimaginable new doors of possibility. Bravo for this work!

Dorothy E. Siminovitch, Ph.D., MCC author of *A Gestalt Coaching Primer: The Path Toward Awareness Intelligence*

If you want to know why metaphors are useful for coaching, there's gold in this book. And if practical examples work better for you, Lyssa's book is rich in examples. There's wisdom here about why metaphor is clear enough, and doesn't need to be pinned down to facts and how it can work across cultures. I love the exploration of how to use metaphor at the start and end of conversations and in checking in. Practical and applicable.'

Claire Pedrick MCC author of *Simplifying Coaching* and *The Human Behind The Coach*

Light Up: The Science of Coaching with Metaphors is a true compendium of resources, research, and references to using metaphors in Coaching conversations. Lyssa's book is invaluable, with clear explanations, skills learned quickly, and multiple resources and examples. You would do well to dive deeper (metaphor) in your coaching &/or personal development by working with and noticing metaphors that show up or can be elicited in the client's situation. Although I've been teaching metaphor use for 20 years, this book is a comprehensive and essential guide for any practitioner's library.

Dr. Patrick Williams, MCC, author of *Getting Naked* and *Becoming a Professional Life Coach*

Lyssa has such a gift for explaining this masterful approach to coaching with metaphors. She does so at great depth and breadth and at the same time with such clarity and simplicity. The extent to which metaphors are enlightened is remarkable and exciting. It's opening up a whole new world for me personally and as a coach. As Lyssa so beautifully describes them, they are "whispers of the soul." This book is the perfect learning adventure. Lyssa shares with us the beauty and magic of metaphors and how to utilize them within the coaching framework and the brain science involved and includes the vital component that drives it all home! She shares examples from real coaching conversations, so we get to experience the work with metaphors in action. We come to understand their vital importance in coaching and how missing them and not working with them is a tragic loss. Indeed, metaphors light up our brains and our lives!

Gail Moore, LMT, RMT, CPC, host of MooreMasterCoaching.com

This book successfully pairs concepts with applications and playfully connects science with art. Lyssa even lets us into her own coaching conversations to help us embody the experience, just like a great metaphor does! Coaches of all experiences will receive valuable insights into not only the power of metaphors but also why they're so important to co-creating dynamic coaching engagements with our clients. The way this book captures it all is brilliant!

Paul Sanbar, PCC, ESIA, builder of the LEGO® SERIOUS PLAY® methods Liminal Spaces™ coaching framework

Light Up, The Science of Coaching with Metaphors is a unique resource for coaches, exploring how metaphors can be an indispensable tool to navigate the landscape of emotions and thoughts, and their profound impact in client interactions. This must-read guide enriches coaching skills by teaching us how to tune our ears to leverage client metaphors as a door to the inner self. Many examples from real coaching conversations bridge the gap between theory and practical application, demonstrating how metaphors can catalyze transformative client journeys. '*Light Up*' is an invaluable resource for coaches who want to expand their ability to be fully present and delve into what really matters."

Lucia Baldelli, MCC, co-author of *The Human Behind The Coach*

Deep beneath the surface of our conversations lies a motherlode of meaning. We speak and think in images that shape our experience of life. Lyssa deHart guides coaches to nimbly engage in conversations that center on the metaphors their clients use. Coaches will learn concrete approaches in *Light Up* that draw on evidence-based lessons from neuroscience, somatic coaching, and a well curated selection of therapeutic modalities. As clients grow accustomed to meeting their own metaphors with curiosity and playfulness, they will unleash bold agency with ease.

Gideon Culman, MCC, Executive Coach at K Street Coaching

At the heart of transformative coaching lies a profound truth: to be heard is fundamental to being coached.

I offer an invitation to coaches who aspire to partner more fully with their clients. By tuning into the unique language of each client and harnessing the power of metaphors, coaches can support clients to unlock deeper insights and illuminate their path forward.

This book is a journey into the art of listening deeply, leveraging language to foster transformation, and having fun.

Happy Coaching!

Light Up
The Science of Coaching with Metaphors

Light Up
The Science of Coaching with Metaphors

Lyssa deHart, LICSW, MCC, BCC

BARN SWALLOW
PUBLISHING
CASCADIA

Light Up
The Science of Coaching with Metaphors

Published by: Barn Swallow Publishing

Address all inquiries to:
Barn Swallow Publishing
BarnSwallowPub@gmail.com

The author of this book is not dispensing medical advice or prescribing the use of any technique as a form of treatment for mental, emotional, physical or medical problems. The reader is responsible for appropriate medical care with their doctor or therapist. The intent of the author is only to offer information to support getting curious about metaphors and how they show up in the work of coaches and therapists. The information is for you alone. The author and the publisher assume no responsibility for how you use the information.

Library of Congress Control Number: 2024900577
Paperback - 978-1-948317-02-3
eBook - 978-1-948317-03-0

Editor: Kirkus Editing Team
Cover Designer: Lyssa deHart
Interior Book Layout: Lyssa deHart
Author Photo: Lyssa deHart
Cover Image and all Art and Diagrams: Lyssa deHart

Every attempt has been made to source properly all research material and quotes.

First Edition :
10 9 8 7 6 5 4 3 2 1

Printed in the United States of America

Contents

This book is affectionately dedicated
to each and every coach & client who has graciously
allowed me to join them on their journey
of learning and growth.

Big Hug.

PREFACE

" I must be a mermaid; I have no fear of depth
and a great fear of shallow living.
—Anaïs Nin, *The Four Chambered Heart*

I became fascinated by metaphors when I noticed them appearing in conversations with my clients. I don't remember what triggered my brain to hold on to their metaphors, but something clicked as I heard these seemingly innocuous turns of phrase. I wasn't sure why, but I believed them to be important. I had the cursory instructions in my coach training to use metaphors, but that tended to be coach-driven. After all, the International Coaching Federation (ICF) core competency seven, 'Evokes Awareness' states, "The coach facilitates client insight and learning by using tools and techniques such as powerful questioning, silence, metaphor, or analogy" (ICF 2019). And to be fair, I loved the way that metaphors sounded and the imagery they invited. I didn't yet know that metaphors had deeper meaning or that they pointed the way toward what was lighting up the client's mind.

As I was beginning to hear how my clients were conceptualizing their experiences, I also noticed that they were much more in sync with their metaphors and less so with the ones I offered. I had been taught to bring metaphors, and although those I offered came from my listening, my metaphors had a tendency to land only some of the time. This became very clear in a coaching demonstration in 2017.

As the client described a difficult and painful relationship with her adult daughter, I heard what sounded like defensiveness, as in she needed to defend herself from her daughter and the painful nature of the relationship. I shared that as she was talking, it sounded like a protective force was covering her, like the Batmobile. "No," she responded. "Not the Batmobile. I see a pink bunny suit."

I never would have come up with that image in a million years. I asked her about the pink bunny suit, and she explained that when her daughter was young, she would dress up with her and wear a pink bunny suit; it was a shared moment of love and laughter between them. She wanted that playfulness when she thought of the conversations she wanted to have with her now-grown daughter. Our coaching conversation was about the movement from disappointment and defensiveness toward a pink bunny suit. This experience was pivotal.

In the context of my work, metaphors are the visual and symbolic expressions used to describe complex internal experiences. Metaphors offer insight into a person's thought patterns, emotions, and perspectives. They serve as a safe bridge for curiosity, exploration, understanding, and meaningful dialogue between the coach and the client. What I realized was that I was being invited into the client's inner landscape. Until then, I had not recognized the invitation.

A Little Backstory

I didn't have your run-of-the-mill upbringing; it was more like a kaleidoscopic journey through a landscape of ideas. My mother, an artist, taught art education at the University of Texas at Austin until she went back to school to become a Jungian psychotherapist. She laid the intellectual foundation of our home. As a kid, I was steeped in conversations and dialogues that went way beyond what was on the dinner menu and how my day was. We talked about those things also, but we'd venture into the realms of philosophy, archetypes, and mythology. I read everything from Dr. Suess and *Winnie the Pooh* to *Man's Search for Meaning* and Joseph Campbell's *The Power of Myth*. My mother was always seeking new ways of thinking and self-awareness, developing her personal philosophy, and forging a spiritual connection with the world. My influences included the Dalai Lama,

Jesus Christ, and the Earth Goddess Gaia. I had many opportunities to explore the human experience from a myriad of lenses.

As I came into my own, I primarily studied art, art history, and anthropology. The exploration of how we as humans developed and became what we are today was fascinating to me. The links amoung art, art history, spirituality, and anthropology were woven together in my mind. The shared human experience through history. The development of language, art, and meaning-making started with the earliest language of imagery. Early cave paintings told stories, and they were tangible evidence of how humans began to describe and share stories of the world around them. The images spoke to the dangers lurking behind rocks and tall grass. Humans were wired for survival, and what was becoming clear was that the brain had developed predictive qualities—specifically for our survival, yes, but our brain also developed the capacity to dream, to wonder, to create, and to share meaning.

My subsequent training in social work refined these broad interests into a focus on trauma and relationships. I delved into a myriad of psychological theories during my graduate studies, ranging from systems and attachment to existential theory. Over time, I built an eclectic therapy practice, drawing on techniques from sand play to EMDR (eye movement desensitization and reprocessing) and psychological theories from person-centered to cognitive behavioral. My aim has always been to guide my clients from dysfunction to functionality, informed by an ever-growing understanding of how our brains are wired—and how they can be rewired.

I draw on this rich background to explore the science of metaphors and the mind, particularly the human capacity for making meaning. As you read, you'll see that my early influences and academic pursuits have greatly shaped the lens through which I view and discuss these issues.

From Therapist to Coach

In coaching, I have discovered that the coach's job is to follow where the client's mind has lit up and partner with them to explore their internal experiences. My bias is that coaches need to approach each session with curiosity and wonder, not assuming that we, the coaches, know the answers but rather assuming that we do not. We can use our expertise to inform our curiosity by asking thought-provoking questions that engage the client's self-awareness and focus on the values underpinning their beliefs, actions, and decisions. The metaphors clients were bringing into conversations became a brilliant way in which to be curious and stay in partnership.

After the pink bunny suit conversation, I started digging into metaphors in a conscious and direct way. My interest only intensified with my research. I taught my first webinar, "Playing with the Power of Metaphors," in August 2018. Metaphors had become a passion for me. Listening for them was a way for me to create strong agreements, build trust and safety, be fully present, listen deeply, evoke awareness, and even facilitate growth in a partnered conversation. It is clear to me that through the lens of metaphors, coaches can be more present and partner more fully with their clients. Listening to and using the client's language was a way to generate deeper self-awareness and ultimately create a safe and playful space in which to explore clients' internal narratives and the meaning they were making from their experiences.

I began to have an issue with the interpretation of the word facilitates, which often means that the coach creates the metaphor for the client rather than tuning their ears to the metaphors clients naturally bring forward in sessions. One way a coach could exemplify missing the metaphor might be when a client would say, "I feel like I'm pushing a boulder up a hill," and the coach would respond, "Yes, it's like a salmon swimming upstream." The coach heard something yet missed the opportunity to use the client's language, creating a disconnect. Now the client needed to stop their thought flow and try to make sense of what the coach had just reinterpreted.

There are many ways a coach might completely miss their clients' metaphors. For example, in one of my early recorded coaching calls*, my conversation went like this:

Client: I would like to talk about starting a business, something

Client: I've immersed myself in lately and am very excited about moving forward with. There are a couple of areas that feel like stumbling blocks to me that I would like to work through. I was hoping to discuss those with you.

Coach: Would you tell me more about your business?

All coaching conversations in this book have been minimally edited for readability.

This led the client to launch into a long explanation about her business ideas, the classes she was taking, and what she hoped to accomplish. With my ears oblivious to the metaphors she offered, I missed the stumbling blocks and instead began facilitating the client so that I could understand how to help her. Her brain was led through an explanatory conversation about details she could have figured out without me. We ultimately got to the meaningful, underlying issue— her lack of confidence—but that could have been uncovered in the first five minutes without her explaining her business plans to me. In short, I took the client into the weeds instead of being curious and led to what was important by her words.

Such scenarios happen daily in thousands of coaching conversations. Clients share metaphors, and a coach is either missing or reinterpreting what they are offering. Both examples demonstrate not listening in partnership.

In that coaching call, my curiosity was focused on understanding a problem and finding a solution. My curiosity was not tuned to partnering with my client or recognizing the invitation into her internal landscape. I had been seduced by the interesting instead of being curious about the important. If I had been curious, the conversation might have gone deeper and ultimately been more useful. If I had Mr. Peabody's Wayback Machine and I could rewrite how I conducted the conversation, here is how I might hope it would have gone:

Client: I would like to talk about starting a business, something I've immersed myself in lately and am very excited about

Client: moving forward with. There are a couple of areas that feel like stumbling blocks to me that I would like to work through.

I was hoping to discuss those with you.

Coach: If we were able to explore and work through these stumbling blocks so that you could move forward, what would be different at the end of our call?

Client: I would have more confidence about moving forward.

Coach: How do you see yourself when you are confident?

Client: Oh, confidence is like that power posing. I can feel it in my body. I'm standing solidly, with one arm up, like I'm getting ready to fly.

Coach: So by the end of this conversation, you will be ready to fly past those stumbling blocks?

Client: Yes! I want to fly over those stumbling blocks!

Coach: Where do you want to begin exploring flying over those stumbling blocks?

In both examples, unknown to me at the time, my client's brain had lit up and was alive in their metaphor of moving forward over those stumbling blocks. In the rewrite, I hear this and get curious about the experience of stumbling blocks and stay with her lit-up brain. What would she prefer? Confidence. What is the experience of confidence? Flying. What would the client want to move toward? To fly over the stumbling blocks. And how would she prefer to explore her relationship with the experience she was having? Partnership in exploring.

When working with a person in a coaching framework, we are always testing hypotheses. We can't know until we ask. These ideas of knowing are based on assumptions. The client said one thing, and the helping professional assumes meaning, focusing all their inquiry on a solution to it. This is how we get stuck in the situational semantics of a conversation. Plus, it sets the conversation in a superficial, top-level, problem-solving exploration while ignoring the deeper currents driving the unconscious narratives, behaviors, or beliefs.

From my experience, behavior is a trailing indicator of an individual's internal experience. To develop understanding and ultimately change behavior, the client needs to light up their brain and explore the inner experience. And although it's nice when our brain, as a coach, lights up too, it's unnecessary for us to hold the container of a coaching conversation. The coach is in a supporting role; participation does not equal partnership. We use curiosity to dive below the waterline, past the iceberg to where the important story and somatic awareness live. Exploring the images that define the experience gives our clients agency drawn from their minds and expertise. Our job is to follow where their brain has lit up.

The need to make sense of someone's internal landscape takes us away from the more profound work of supporting them to make their own sense. Instead of coming into conversations as the expert or the assumed expert, we might invite ourselves to coach in the space of not knowing and being full of wonder. We open ourselves to be novices to the clients' expertise and allow ourselves to be taught by and to learn from them as they share with us their internal experiences. We have an opportunity to hold the space for discovery. All we know can be used to inform our curiosity, then rinse, wash, and repeat as we test our hypotheses in the form of inquiry for the benefit of the client's awareness and clarity.

In many ways, coaching, at its best, follows the Socratic method of inquiry. It is neither teaching nor telling, per se. It is not a lecture or the transference of knowledge to the client. The coach is neither the expert nor the wise sage, sharing wisdom for client growth. Your clients are not passive recipients of your knowledge. The Socratic method involves a shared dialogue between the client and the coach, with both asking thought-provoking questions that engage the client's self-awareness. The focus is not on the client's situation but on the value system that underpins their beliefs, actions, and decisions.

The Anaïs Nin quote at the beginning of this preface illustrates my experience of this. I see all my clients as gender-neutral mermaids. My job is to dive below the waterline with curiosity and explore what shows up. We coach in deep waters. And I love doing this with the playfulness and depth that metaphors invite.

How This Might Sound in a Coaching Session

Your client has come to the session frazzled. Somewhere in their immediate download of the day, you hear them say, "I am over-whelmed." They have said more than that, but the overarching theme is overwhelm, so you begin coaching.

The coaching exploration is not about solving the overwhelm, as these typical responses imply: "You need to breathe." "Overwhelm is normal." "May I lead you through this relaxation exercise?" "Do you think you're being hard on yourself?" "I would be overwhelmed too if I had all that going on."

The coaching exploration involves getting curious about what overwhelm means to the client, what they would like to be different, and what they learn about themselves as they share what is between the meaning and the outcome. As the client clarifies the overwhelm—what it is, what it isn't, what is different when they are not overwhelmed, how their thinking shifts, or how their body feels—they learn about themselves through inquiry. From this learning, they are able to decide how they might want to experience their situation differently. Ultimately, they are digging into why they are presently experiencing their situation this way and moving toward how they would like to experience it—not feeling overwhelmed. This is where metaphors invite us to be more playfully and creatively explore meaning, giving the client the clarity of distance in the exploration and developing actions aligned with insight.

Client: I have so much going on right now. I have this huge
           project at work, and my teenager is driving me crazy.
           I feel like I can't take one more drop of water in my
           bucket. I am so overwhelmed with my life right now.

Coach: I hear that your bucket can't take another drop.

Client: It's like an overflowing bucket, and I am constantly splashing over the edges.

Coach: How would you rather experience your bucket?

Client: I would rather stop adding water to my bucket and drain some of the water so that there's room at the top and I'm not constantly splashing over the edges.

Coach: What's different when you have room at the top of your bucket?

Client: I feel calm and balanced. I have space to breathe and don't feel so frantic about everything.

Coach: Just to clarify, in our conversation today, would it be useful to explore the idea of creating space at the top of your bucket?

Client: Yes. I want to have space in the bucket, and I also want to feel more peace in my life.

Coach: Where do we begin in this exploration toward that peaceful space at the top of your bucket?

In this context, the coach recognizes the critical underlying issue of "overwhelm," but instead of assuming understanding and pushing the client toward a solution without exploration, the coach begins testing the hypothesis of the client's meaning and metaphorical interpretation of their experience. "I am overwhelmed. Overwhelm is like water splashing over the bucket's edge. I want to stop adding water and drain the bucket. I feel calm and peaceful when I have space at the top of my bucket." In a coaching conversation, we are getting clarity and alignment about what is important to the client—peace and space at the top of the bucket—and we partner with the client when we ask how they would like to dive into the bucket.

Ultimately, the solutions the client will generate as worth following through on will come from the clarity and understanding of what is driving the overwhelm. Let's say that through exploring this overfull bucket, the client discovers that they need to set healthy boundaries on their time. Or that they need to stop saying yes because they don't want their teenager to be angry with them. Now they have started to create and connect some dots. They have a brimming bucket. They don't enjoy it when it's so full, and they need space at the top. They are saying yes to things because they are avoiding the discomfort of people being mad at them, so they need to set some healthier boundaries.

Toward the end of the conversation, the coach can support the client in anchoring or grounding their learning and ask questions that help them determine actions that come from the insights created in the conversation. If asked, clients naturally come up with actions aligned with what they have discovered: "I need to prioritize the things I am doing and then renegotiate agreements with people." Or "I will slow down my yes to a maybe and take a bit more time before I decide." Or "I will check in with my teen and explore what might work for both of us and not just say yes to avoid a difficult conversation." Or all of the above. When the client creates the actions from their insights, more often than not, they follow through on those self-determined actions. Again, this is how partnership looks. The coach listens deeply, holds the space for insights, and then supports the client's agency in self-determined actions.

My Hope

This book will examine how we became wired for metaphors. We will explore the theories and science behind conceptual metaphors, discussing the value of client-led conversations and embodied cognition. I will share many examples from real coaching conversations to show how tuning your ears to hear and then leveraging metaphors that light up your client's mind might deepen your conversations. This will provide you with greater partnership in your coaching as you support your clients in achieving sustainable outcomes and success in accomplishing their goals.

My ultimate goal is for you, the coach, to have more access to working with the metaphors your clients share with you. I want you to expand your ability to be fully present with and hear their words, be wholly curious, and support them to explore the deeper and often more important issues that reside below the surface. I hope you come to have better results and a lot more fun with your clients as you have crucial coaching conversations.

Chapter 1: Your Brain & Visual Language

" Your vision will become clear only when you can look into
your own heart. Who looks outside, dreams;
who looks inside, awakes.
—Carl Jung, Letter to Fanny Bowditch, 22 October 1916

In this chapter, we will explore the role of visual language in the brain and how it connects to metaphors. Metaphors are like a bridge between the worlds of language and images, linking the words we speak with the pictures we see in our mind's eye. Research in linguistics has shown that when we hear or read a metaphor, our brains activate the same areas that are responsible for processing visual information. That is because, at its core, a metaphor is a way of using language to create a mental image.

Think of it this way: Our brains are wired with a network of visual neurons that are constantly looking for patterns and connections. When we encounter a metaphor, these neurons light up like fireworks, pairing the words we hear with the images they represent. This is why metaphors have the power to transport us to new places, why they can be so evocative and memorable. They literally light up our minds.

Metaphors are like a secret passageway that lets us access the visual parts of our brain, enabling us to see the world in new and exciting ways. They are powerful tools that let us explore the depths of our imagination, to experience the world from our own unique lens.

Consider for a moment each of the following bullet points. Close your eyes and see what they mean to you.

- I am wrestling with this situation.
- I see the path; I don't know the steps to get on it.
- I keep hitting a wall.
- When my boundaries get pushed, I wrap myself in armor.

In each statement, you can picture the speaker struggling with something or trying to imagine a way forward. This is the power of visual language. We experience the words.

The Hemispheres of the Brain

Research into the neuroscience of metaphors has revealed that both hemispheres of the brain are involved in the process of understanding metaphors. The right hemisphere exhibits flexibility, managing a variety of metaphorical and literal primes, whereas the left hemisphere retains a precise sense of metaphor without interference from alternate meanings. In this context, "primes" refer to instances of metaphor use that prepare the brain for comprehension—they are the subtle clues that ready the brain to interpret the meaning of words or ideas. This study also suggests that metaphor comprehension is dynamic: the right hemisphere is adaptable to new contexts, and the left hemisphere exhibits nuanced processing. (Chettih et al. 2012).

Further, metaphor comprehension is recognized as a cognitively complex task involving multiple brain areas. The right hemisphere's involvement seems to vary depending on the cognitive effort required, hinting at a nuanced role that depends on the complexity of the task and potentially on the novelty or familiarity of the metaphor (Duque et al. 2023).

Functional neuroimaging studies have implicated both hemispheres when processing and understanding metaphors, challenging the traditional notion that the right hemisphere is solely responsible for this function (Cardillo et al. 2012). The role of the right hemisphere in metaphor comprehension has been a subject of debate, with some neuroimaging studies indicating that factors like the conventionality of the metaphor, the sentential context, and the cognitive demands of the task can influence the right hemisphere's involvement.

These studies suggest that the interaction between the right hemisphere, which may contribute more to the creative and novel aspects of metaphor comprehension, and the left hemisphere, which handles the linguistic and semantic processing, is complex and dynamic and not necessarily well understood yet. The cognitive load (i.e., cognitive complexity and familiarity of the metaphor) may play a significant role in determining the extent of each hemisphere's involvement (Duque et al. 2023).

Visual Focus

Most cultures describe five primary senses: sight, taste, touch, hearing, and smell. We depend on these external senses to feed us information. As we move into meaning-making, these senses become the foundation of how we formulate understanding. Although every living creature has senses, how strongly they manifest is unique to each species. For example, consider the sense of smell. A dog can draw epic amounts of information from a fire hydrant; humans, not so much. That said, you might delight in the smell of warm cookies fresh from the oven or the woodsy smoke from a fire on a chilly night.

Although you use all your senses to varying degrees, human evolution has spent a lot of energy on the sense of vision. The brain itself has hundreds of millions of neurons devoted to visual processing. Approximately 55 percent of the cortex's neurons are specialized for this task, compared with 3 percent for auditory processing and 11 percent for somatosensory processing (Felleman and Van Essen 1991). Interestingly, 90 percent of the information transmitted to the brain is visual due to this ability to parse out incredible amounts of information. "Because half of the human brain is devoted directly or indirectly to vision, understanding the process of vision provides clues to understanding fundamental operations in the brain" (Massachusetts Institute of Technology 1997).

There is no veracity to the 3M meme that we process visual

images sixty thousand times faster than text. Literally, there is no research. Yet we anecdotally understand that we process visual information much more quickly. Ask any marketer if an ad with only words works as well as an ad with a fantastic image. Consider the "Got Milk?" ads. Those work because the marketers spent years showing us milk mustaches or Moostaches on every conceivable celebrity from Dennis Rodman to the Simpsons and people trying to eat a dry cookie; oh, the inhumanity! The imagery is primed in your mind: milk. When you think of cookies soon to come out of the oven, you remember how much better they taste with a cold glass of milk as you cuddle up by that warm fire.

The retina of the eye contains 150 million light-sensitive rods and cones; that retina is actually an outgrowth of the brain. Each of the body's two optic nerves carries signals from the retina to the brain and consists of 1 million fibers—yes, 1 million. Each auditory nerve carries a mere thirty thousand. The brain has devoted many resources to the ability to perceive the world through visual mediums (Grady 2019).

A 1998 study using college students at the University of Toronto found more activity in the medial temporal cortex when the participants were looking at (encoding) pictures rather than words (Grady et al. 1998). This suggests that images more directly or effectively engage these memory-related regions in the brain, resulting in superior recollection of visual imagery. In short, human beings remember pictures better than words. We will return to this in chapter 11 when we discuss metaphors in coaching conversations.

A 2018 study suggested that blind individuals' comprehension of metaphorical expressions does not differ from that of sighted participants (Minervino et al. 2018). Regardless of their inability to see, blind people fully experience the world around them. They understand the idea of rain clouds, as they ostensibly have walked in the rain and felt the air becoming colder as the clouds darken, and they have likely heard people remark, "Those are dark clouds." So the metaphorical meaning of saying "I have a dark cloud over my head" would not be lost on a blind person.

This is conjecture on my part, but a blind person being coached might tend to refer to the other senses in metaphorical meaning-making. They might use moving, eating, and manipulating metaphors over visual ones. Yet, that said, people who don't have sight still have brains, and although they do not see in the same way as a sighted person, they still fully sense their world and use metaphorical idea containers to share meaning.

Putting It into Perspective

The brain has placed a lot of importance on vision, and because the brain is fundamentally designed to support survival, the senses that help us survive are hardwired. As we explore conceptual metaphors, remember that the structures in the brain developed to help you survive. As proposed by Lisa Feldman Barrett (2020), we must understand that the organ's primary function is to regulate and maintain the body's essential functions for survival. Simply put, your brain lights up in different areas that are aligned with the structures that evolved to help humans survive.

When we dive into the realm of conceptual metaphors, we see these survival-oriented structures in the brain at work. The brain is predictive and evolved to react to immediate physical needs, anticipate future needs, and learn from past experiences.

Conceptual metaphors are part of this complex cognitive function. They create bridges between abstract ideas and concrete experiences, enabling us to understand and communicate complex thoughts and emotions. In a nutshell, metaphors point to the open doorway the mind has created to explain and make meaning of the experience.

Regardless of which side of the brain is involved, metaphors are the paintbrush of the mind, allowing us to create vivid pictures with our words to explain our internal narrative or schema. In this book, *schema* refers to an individual's mental framework or blueprint that organizes and interprets information, shaping their perception and understanding of the world. Metaphorically speaking, as we paint pictures with words, we create idea containers to share the deeper meaning with others. And, fundamentally, as we are a social species, sharing meaning is essential to a person's ability to interact with other people and thus to survive.

Questions

- How does the brain process metaphors, and what connections does this process have with visual imagery?

- Reflect on the studies mentioned in the chapter. How do they suggest visual metaphors impact memory and comprehension, even in the absence of sight?

- How do our five senses contribute to our understanding and creation of metaphors, with a particular focus on vision?

- Based on your understanding of this chapter, how do metaphors serve as a tool for survival and social interaction?

- What is your biggest takeaway from this chapter?

Reading Recommendation

Seven and a Half Lessons about the Brain by Lisa Feldman Barrett

Chapter 2: Conceptual Metaphors

" Our ordinary conceptual system, in terms of which we both think and act, is fundamentally metaphorical in nature.

—George Lakoff and Mark Johnson, *Metaphors We Live By*

Metaphors have been around since humans needed to explain anything more complex than how to boil water. The word *metaphor* comes from the Greek word μεταφορά (metaphorá), meaning "transference" (of ownership) (Liddell and Scott 1901). Metaphors are idea containers that take one idea and transfer meaning to another idea.

The idea of conceptual metaphor as an area of study began in the field of linguistics. Linguists studied metaphors not only as a turn of phrase but also as an important way to communicate complex ideas. The research began in earnest in the 1970s by cognitive linguists Michael Reddy, George Lakoff, and Mark Johnson. Lakoff and Johnson's book *Metaphors We Live By*, which was published in 1980, was seminal in exploring how people use metaphors. What was becoming apparent was that people used them to more vividly share experiences as complex thoughts, such as the idea of falling in love with no actual falling involved. However, the experience is understood as someone coming to be in love with another.

These authors were studying language and how people use it to communicate complex ideas in nonliteral ways. "The essence of metaphor is understanding and experiencing one kind of thing in terms of another" (Lakoff and Johnson 1980, 5). They demonstrated that metaphors were not unique and rarely used idioms, they discovered that everyday people used metaphors regularly in everyday language. The words themselves are not important but rather the ideas the words carry.

Through what he calls conduit metaphors, Michael Reddy (1979) found that the novel abstract concepts of communication and ideas are understood via conceptual metaphors:

- Ideas are objects.
- Language is a container for idea-objects.
- Communication is sending idea-objects in language containers.

Reddy's idea is that if someone is communicating to you metaphorically, that person is putting an idea-object into an idea container and sending it to you. The meaning is being carried through the language of another thing. When someone says, "I feel like I am pushing a boulder up a hill," we will all agree that the person is not actually pushing a boulder. But you probably understand that they are communicating that they are working hard and maybe not getting very far.

Lakoff said about Reddy, "The contemporary theory that metaphors are primarily conceptual, conventional, and part of the ordinary system of thought and language can be traced to Michael Reddy's now classic essay . . . With a single, thoroughly analyzed example, he allowed us to see, albeit in a restricted domain, that ordinary everyday English is largely metaphorical, dispelling once and for all the traditional view that metaphor is primarily in the realm of poetic or 'figurative' language. Reddy showed, for a single, very significant case, that the locus of metaphor is thought, not language, that metaphor is a major and indispensable part of our ordinary, conventional way of conceptualizing the world, and that our everyday behavior reflects our metaphorical understanding of experience. Though other theorists had noticed some of these characteristics of metaphor, Reddy was the first to demonstrate them by rigorous linguistic analysis, stating generalizations over voluminous examples" (Lakoff 1993, 203).

Let me repeat this: The locus of metaphor is thought, not language. They are a major and indispensable part of ordinary ways of conceptualizing the world. This is crucial for a coach to understand. The metaphors a client shares with the coach are a window into their thinking.

Researchers have broken metaphors into categories such as novel and dead/frozen. A novel metaphor is a new or original metaphor that has not been used before or, at the very least, has not been used frequently. It can effectively make language more engaging and vivid and help communicate ideas in a fresh and interesting way.

On the other hand, a dead/frozen metaphor is one that has become so common and familiar that it is no longer perceived as a metaphor. These are heard as common, literal expressions. They are often so common that they are almost invisible to speakers of the language and may not even be recognized as metaphors by many people.

Examples of dead metaphors in English include *grasp the concept, break the news, see the light, and take the plunge.* These phrases are all metaphorical, but they are so common and familiar that they are no longer perceived as such by many people. Another example is *things are coming to a head,* where the original meaning was lost on most speakers and listeners, given that when events are coming to a head, we are not thinking about popping pimples, yet that is what the phrase was originally meant to capture.

The General Theory Began Evolving

From the work of Eve Sweetser and Alan Schwartz in the late 1970s and early 1980s, conceptual metaphors began to have more clarity.

They linked language to the body. Physical elements mattered to the expression of metaphor. The ideas of manipulation, perceiving, moving, and eating came from the mind, linguistic, and somatic expression.

The use of metaphors lit up the regions of the brain associated with the different areas of movement, vision, manipulation, and eating.

There are four main areas of conceptual metaphors:

1. *Thinking is moving*: Ideas are locations we move through; communicating is leading; understanding is following.

2. *Thinking is seeing*: Ideas are things seen; communication is showing.

3. *Thinking is object manipulation*: Ideas are objects; communication is sending; understanding is grasping.

4. *Thinking is eating*: Ideas are food; communication is feeding; understanding is digesting.

Here are some examples for each:

- *Thinking is moving*: Reach a decision; capture your thoughts; I'm going off topic; are you following me? I'm lost in the weeds.

- *Thinking is seeing*: That's an enlightened perspective; it's my point of view; we'll shed light on that; I was blinded by love; see what I mean?

- *Thinking is manipulating*: I'm turning it over in my mind; let me toss these ideas around; I find myself wrestling with my fear.

- *Thinking is eating*: Food for thought; let's digest that idea; my plate is full.

From an anthropological perspective, these findings align with the elements of brain development that early humans would have needed to survive as they navigated their environment, as discussed earlier. The senses come into play as well. The conceptual metaphors follow along with the brain functions that developed as humans became tool users and the most successfully manipulative mammals on the planet. The areas of sight, movement, manipulation, and food are hardwired into the human brain.

From Lakoff and Johnson's (1980) work, we fold into this process that a way we create meaning is through image schema. We comprehend abstract ideas through sensory images (pictures in our minds). Thus, when we hear a word like open, we recognize that it might be speaking about a literal door being open, yet it isn't a stretch for us to imagine the opening of our mind or the opening of opportunities. Similarly, we also experience the closing of minds, doors, and opportunities. Furthermore, we create mental images to make sense of these openings and closings. We all use these image schemas to translate our inner experiences and meaning into understandable ideas for others.

Novel conceptual metaphors light up correlating regions of the human brain. Thousands of embodied metaphor mapping circuits make up their structure. These mapping circuits asymmetrically link distinct brain regions, allowing reasoning patterns from one brain region to apply to another (Lakoff 2014).

James Geary said, "Whenever we describe anything abstract: ideas, feelings, thoughts, emotions, concepts, we instinctively resort to metaphors." To put some contextual flesh on this statement, describe an experience you've had involving a powerful emotion like passion, overwhelm, or confusion:

_____

_____

_____

_____

Most people will share metaphorically what that experience of these emotions feels like to them.

For example, let's play with passion. "Passion is when I am flooded with desire and swept off my feet." Rarely will you get a response that sounds like this: "Passion feels like an intense desire to have something or someone." Literally, that may be true, but most people will use the language of metaphors, and if a coach asks one more question—"How do you experience intense desire?"—the answer will probably become metaphorical.

Human experiences are similar across cultures. We all feel joy, hardship, confusion, love, passion, and many other related elements of the overarching human condition; metaphor maps work in most brains. The metaphors may sound different, and how we communicate ideas is unique to our language and cultural contexts, as metaphors are learned experientially through conversations and cultural meaning. However, all cultures use metaphors.

Dead and/or Frozen Metaphors

As mentioned earlier, dead metaphors, often referred to as frozen or conventional metaphors, are phrases so embedded in our language that they no longer spark surprise or vivid imagery, yet they have the potential to be very much alive. Originating from the linguistic concept where these metaphors blend into everyday speech, they become indistinguishable from ordinary expressions. However, as discussed by Lakoff and Johnson (1980), they are far from extinct in our cognitive landscape. Instead, they operate subconsciously, embedded in well-trodden phrases that still carry profound but unconscious meaning for the speaker.

Examples of these metaphors in conversations could include phrases like the following: "I want to lean into feedback," "I have mixed feelings about my child leaving for college," "I am feeling stuck about next steps," "I keep rewinding the conversation," "I want to dive into this new position," or "I need to give myself more wiggle room." Their frequent use has led to a certain immunity, dulling our sensitivity to their potential deeper implications.

In the realms of coaching and therapy, recognizing and understanding these dead metaphors is crucial. Overlooking them means missing out on rich layers of meaning in our client interactions. It also means that we miss opportunities. Despite some coaches believing that their clients don't employ metaphors, deep listening often reveals their pervasive presence in conversations. By tuning into these seemingly mundane expressions, we can uncover a wealth of possible opportunities to test that might lead to insights and deepen clarity for our clients as they navigate their experience.

Missed Opportunities

Metaphors show up in both therapy and coaching. "The therapeutic relevance of this is clear: If metaphors are important in structuring our thoughts about ourselves and the world, and act as filters that regulate how we view our present and our past—as claimed by Siegelman in his book 'Metaphor and Meaning in Psychotherapy'— they can be an important target of therapy" (Malkomsen et al. 2022, 2).

Metaphors are a significant aspect of cognitive behavioral therapy (CBT) and are often incorporated into CBT training. In their work on CBT and metaphors, Richard Stott and colleagues (2010) emphasize how metaphors serve as a crucial link, connecting abstract concepts with tangible examples in CBT. The authors found that therapists provided a variety of metaphors for educational purposes, such as likening worrying thoughts to quicksand. I see the same thing in the hundreds of coaching conversations I have listened to in coach training, where the coach is trained to bring the metaphor, typically to highlight something or for teaching purposes.

This idea of the therapist or the coach bringing the metaphor, in my experience, is problematic. This practice of leading the client with our metaphors may speak to why many therapists and coaches have ambivalent feelings about using metaphors. When the coach or therapist brings the metaphor, they are not deeply listening to what the client is offering, and they are potentially contaminating the space with their perspective and meaning-making. Thankfully, when there is enough trust, clients redirect both therapists and coaches.

"Most therapists said that they do not actively listen for metaphors in therapy, and many said that they seldom use metaphors deliberately" (Malkomsen et al. 2022, 1). I don't think coaches are that different, and, in my perspective, it is a huge missed opportunity.

Source and Target Domains

I am covering this section in broad strokes, as this is a rabbit hole that is infinitely deep. Zoltán Kövecses (Kövecses, 2010) writes about the differences between conceptual and linguistic metaphors in his research. He gives the example of a linguistic metaphor as a turn of phrase that doesn't convey a deeper meaning. For example, coaches need open minds and hearts, or I want you to tune your ears to metaphors. The language is metaphorical. In these examples, there is no deeper concept being explained. The language is used poetically. When you consider conceptual metaphors, all that changes; they may be poetic, but they are trying to communicate something much more complex.

From a coaching perspective, we are listening not for every metaphor a person uses but rather for the ones that might communicate something deeper. To do this, let's add to the four conceptual metaphors that started the way we use metaphors in modern times and then explore the idea of source and target domains. Conceptual metaphors often have a concrete concept as the source and an abstract one as the target. If I said at a wedding, "I have a full plate," it might imply that I took too much food from the buffet. However, the same thing said in a conversation with someone about their overfull schedule has a very different target.

Source: Concrete Concept	Target: Abstract Concept
Overflowing plate	Overwhelmed

This concrete container for an abstract idea is what I am listening for as a coach, as my clients tell me what they want to work on in our conversation. I am listening for the novel metaphors that contain important abstract concepts that paint a picture of how they perceive of and function in their lives and in the world. Some universal underlying topics tend to run through most people's life experiences.

Common sources that most metaphors use are the human body, movement/direction, manipulation, food/eating, seeing, hearing, birth/death, nature/plants, pathways, sports, buildings, machines, hot/cold, light/dark, light/heavy, obstacles, and forces.

Common targets in metaphors that a coach might pay particular attention to include emotion, desire/wants, morality, thought, society, human relationships, communication, time, life and death, spirituality, and taking action.

From my experience as a therapist, I witnessed that people tend to have some underlying themes they bring to coaching. These themes or ideas are fairly universal and seem to flow around things like meaning/purpose, hopes/dreams, expectations, appreciation, acknowledgment, ethical/moral elements, integrity, trust, balance, important values, boundaries, autonomy/control, safety/threat, commitment, grace, love/hate, growth, life directions, relationships with self and others, and beginnings and endings.

These are not exhaustive lists, but they give you some idea about what important topics your clients may bring up and the underlying target concepts that might be relevant in considering what someone is talking about metaphorically.

Let's look at some examples:

Metaphor	Source: Concrete Concept	Target: Abstract Concept	Possible Underlying Theme
I'm fried	Being cooked	Feeling burnt out	Burn out, tired

Metaphor	Source: Concrete Concept	Target: Abstract Concept	Possible Underlying Theme
My relationship has hit a dead end.	Dead end on a road or path	The ending of a relationship	Endings, grief, closure
I give everyone else wiggle room, but I never give the same wiggle room to myself.	Wiggle room	Flexibility in expectations, grace	Being hard on oneself
I am a very rooted person, and I want my family to have a place to grow.	Rooted, how plants are anchored in the soil	Stability, a sense of well-being; a nurturing environment	The importance of safety and security for the family
I want to explore some of the stumbling blocks in my path as I start this new business.	Stumbling blocks	Challenges	What's in the way of a new beginning
I am running a marathon, and I never cross the finish line.	Running a marathon; Crossing the finish line	Difficulty in completing an important task that feels endless	Integrity, finishing what we start; being disappointed in oneself; shame

I am not saying 100 percent that these are the source, target, or underlying themes. Instead, they are hypotheses that I want to test. I want to get curious about with my client. People constantly surprise me with new and different ways that they express the deeper workings of their experiences. Meaning is unique; I may hear it one way, and the client may mean it in another.

As a coach, I need to set my assumptions aside. I typically, without more detail, riff off what the client shared. I don't need to stop their mental flow and ask for the specific meaning—for example, "When you say, 'Plate,' I hear overwhelm. What do you hear?" Asking for meaning here is unnecessary, as the client already knows what they mean by full plate, and the coach can trust that and ask instead, "What would you like to do with this full plate?" Follow where the client's brain has lit up to take you.

Circling back to the pink bunny suit conversation, remember that when talking to my client, the mother, conversations between her and her daughter often felt fraught with dangerous places, where feelings easily got hurt. As she shared this story, I tested a hypothesis. "This feels a little like the Batmobile, with all the armor coming up." My hypothesis was wrong. She responded, "No, that image doesn't work for me at all. I need a pink bunny suit." As we talked about the pink bunny suit, it was clear that it represented a time in her relationship with her daughter when things were fun and light. She wanted to explore what allowed her to wear the metaphorical pink bunny suit with her daughter now.

The point here is that we need to hold our understanding of meaning or assumptions lightly, with open hands, ready to release any attachment at a moment's notice. Because the client understands that the link from bunny suit equals ease of relationship, we can let ourselves be led as we follow what is lighting up her mind.

Source: Concrete Concept	Target: Abstract Concept
Pink bunny suit	Having fun and connecting with daughter

If I had not tested my incorrect hypothesis of the Batmobile with nonattachment, we wouldn't have gotten to the beautiful idea container of the pink bunny suit. We might have stayed in the story of her and her daughter's complicated relationship and the heavy sadness she felt instead of exploring what allowed her to show up with light and loving energy.

Hypothesis Testing

Clients bring up a lot of metaphors in conversations. In their study, Fiona Mathieson and colleagues (2016) found that people used between seventeen and forty-nine metaphors per one thousand words. In another estimation, people use about six metaphors a minute (Tosey et al. 2013), with some of them being novel and others being the dead or frozen metaphors we discussed earlier (Pollio et al. 1977).

It is difficult to provide an exact number of how many metaphors the average person uses in a conversation, as this can vary greatly depending on the person, the context of the discussion, and the language being spoken. Some people use metaphors more frequently in their everyday language while others use them less often. The point is that humans use metaphors a lot. Coaches who try to grab them all will find themselves hopping all over the place, overwhelmed, and probably confused. That is not the point of listening for metaphors.

Learn to pay attention to the conceptual metaphors that have the source-target-theme that seems important and then begin testing your hypothesis. How do you determine what metaphor is important to the client? Simply ask your client to go back to one of the sources/targets discussed earlier. "I am hearing you talk about giving yourself more wiggle room. That sounds important. What does giving yourself more wiggle room mean to you?" In this inquiry, a coach asks and tests the hypothesis that this might be important and explores what it means with no assumptions of said value, meaning, or importance. The client is able to direct the coach: "This is what it means to me. It is important. The wiggle room is the grace I want to give myself—the willingness to give myself space and not to be perfect."

You don't have to discuss being perfect or the complications of perfectionism, which might lead down a path of negative self-judgment: "I should stop being a perfectionist." Instead, by exploring the metaphor, you use your understanding to inform your curiosity as you invite the client to explore through the conduit of wiggle room. That is a setup for a profound conversation: What does giving wiggle room look like? How do you give it to others? What is the experience of giving wiggle room to yourself? What lets you wiggle more? The questions are endless; they have the potential to bring creative curiosity into the conversation while still doing real work. All through the exploration of the metaphor.

Questions

- If metaphors are a way of carrying and transferring ideas, can you think of a time when one helped you understand a difficult concept better? What was the metaphor, and why did it work for you?

- What are the common source and target domains in metaphors that a coach might pay attention to? Write down some examples of metaphors using these domains.

- When your client uses a metaphor, how conscious are you of its underlying themes or concepts?

- What is an example from your coaching of testing a hypothesis in a conversation?

- What is your biggest takeaway from this chapter?

Reading Recommendation

Metaphors We Live By by George Lakoff and Mark Johnson

Chapter 3: Owned Metaphors

> " When a tree falls in a lonely forest, and no animal is nearby to hear it, does it make a sound?

—Charles Riborg Mann and George Ransom Twiss, *Physics*

Listen for the whispers of the soul. That's what I call owned metaphors, those internal experiences that are expressed through language. These words hold the key to unlocking a deeper understanding of your client's thoughts and emotions. Unlike disowned metaphors, which focus on external experiences, owned metaphors typically start with *I* or *my*. They bring the client's inner world to the surface, revealing the internal experience that drives their behavior.

Think of these phrases as invitations to delve deeper: "I'm on the fence," "I'm at a crossroads," "I'm wrestling with this issue." Each one paints a picture of what's going on in your client's mind. As a coach, it's your job to listen carefully and to ask questions that help your client explore their experience. "I hear you're on the fence. What would be different if you were no longer on the fence?" Or "What about the fence would you want to explore today?"

Your client is bringing themselves into their image schema through a metaphor. By listening for and engaging with these owned metaphors, you can help them navigate the complexities of their inner world. Empower them to find their own solutions and help them grow into the best version of themselves. Listen closely and let your curiosity be your guide. The whispers of the soul are waiting to be heard.

Unconsciously Said, Intentionally Used

The question that opened this chapter, roughly—If a tree falls in a forest and nobody is there to hear it, did it make a sound?—illuminates the importance of the coach's capacity to listen. People don't use metaphors consciously; they use them with *unconscious intentionality*. You don't structure an explanation of an idea with conscious attention to the metaphors you are going to use. The metaphors effortlessly flow from your mind. Yet, from this unconscious state, the metaphors are a conduit for the listener/coach to hear the inner workings of the speaker's mind. The meaning individuals will make of the metaphor is unique to them, but these conceptual metaphors invite all manner of places to be curious and ultimately allow for greater insight and self-awareness. If the coach doesn't hear the metaphor, the client doesn't anchor it as a way through the exploration.

Here is an example of a coaching conversation:

Coach: What is coming to the surface for you for coaching today?

Client: We have an offer to move to a bigger house, and it's right next door to where we live now. But this is the fourth time that our neighbor offered this. She's a very sweet lady; we're very close, and she's like family. She's an older woman, and her kids don't help her, so she wants to downsize.

But before I get my hopes up, I need to think about a few things. The kids would have their own space. I would have my own office, and I really like that idea. But in the past, she's gone back and forth. "I'm ready . . . I'm not ready." And then I'm like, "Well, that's crap, you know?"

We rent our house right now, and we're getting in a position to buy. Something I've learned about myself is that I'm a deeply rooted person, like very deeply rooted.

We've lived in this house for five years, and I know everybody's like, "You could have paid a house partially down for that." And I get it. I love our street; I love our neighborhood. And that's one of the reasons why it's hard to want to move anywhere else because of the connections and our neighborhood. We have so many friends, and our kids play together with our neighbors' kids. So the idea of moving next door is really cool.

I don't know why I'm so uncertain, because it would be nice to have the bigger space, but I've put so much sweat equity and money into my front yard because I thought we'd be here for a little while. And so yesterday this happened. She came and said, "I'm serious this time. I'm ready. I want to downsize, and I want to put my house on the market in the next few weeks."

Coach: Can I stop you for just one second? You've brought up a really big topic, but I feel like there's something deeply rooted under it. What is important for us to explore?

In this example, the client isn't cognizant that she is using the language of being a deeply rooted person. It's the way she unconsciously conceptualizes herself. As the coach, I hear a download around buying a house and moving next door. Yet when the client talks about herself, the metaphors surface. It doesn't matter which conceptual metaphor group this fits into. What matters is that it is an owned metaphor, not a random one: "I am a deeply rooted person." This is important. All the other stuff is filler, and while interesting, the neighbor wanting to downsize is the situation.

For the coach, there is a choice point. Do I ask, "Can you share more about what is important about moving?" Or do I begin getting curious about the idea container of the client being deeply rooted? Do I use the client's language to explore what is meaningful and important? To move or not to move is the situation, but it isn't important to what is driving the internal conflict. The struggle in moving is an external representation of the internal experience of not wanting to lose the rooted feeling. The client doesn't need a coach to walk her through a decision tree; she needs to explore what is below the surface. What does it mean to her to be rooted? A coach can invite her below the waterline, to the parts of the iceberg where the explorations will ultimately support her actions and results.

The Art of Listening

Have you ever found yourself stuck in a repetitive pattern of thoughts and experiences? I believe we all have a habit of sharing our experiences in familiar ways. We may take on different roles, such as the victim, the hero, the helper, or the challenger, and our stories become codified in our minds. But as we continue to mull over our experiences, we may no longer hear what we're saying with curiosity.

If I am coming to you as my coach, sharing a story about what's going on in my life, I probably have a way of sharing that story that is partially habit. And as I relay it to you, I may no longer hear it from outside my internalized echo chamber.

For example, let's say you're in a long-term relationship. You probably don't need the other person in order to argue with them in your mind. You will say X, they will say Y, and, as your coach, I will respond with Z. Our brain habituates almost everything. Habits, even in thoughts, save the brain energy. Remember our discussion in the last chapter on Barrett's work on the brain as a body-budgeting system? Your brain will always attempt to save energy. You never know when you will need it to survive. So when people tell their story, they share it by rote, no longer hearing what they are saying. That's where coaching and therapy come in. Reflection is powerful in that we hear ourselves in new ways when we are heard by others.

Rote reflection is what many coaches do: "I hear you say you love your neighborhood, you're settled, the lady next door has come to you again and offered that she might be ready to sell you her house, and now you are finding yourself confused over what to do."

1. This type of reflection is a lot of work for the coach, as you need to try to pull together all the conversation topics and remember them over several minutes.

2. Many coaches will latch on to what sounds most important to them. Thus, they begin leading the conversation: "Let's talk about what would stop you from moving."

3. The reflection restates what the client just said, demonstrating listening, but it's for the coach, not the client. Most coaches are really trying to make sure they understand the context.

Listening is a powerful tool in coaching, and reflecting on what we've heard is crucial to this skill. Verbatim restating is a technique often used in conflict resolution and marriage therapy, where couples are encouraged to slow down and truly demonstrate that they have listened to each other. But let's be honest: Most coaching conversations aren't arguments; they're about curiosity and moving forward. You have the opportunity to learn to craft your questions and reflections with more partnership and with a touch of creativity, finesse, and fun.

Artful Reflection

Listening for the owned metaphors shines in artful reflection. The coach shares the themes and threads they heard by reflecting the metaphor that the client used. The coach may be naming possible underlying issues such as overwhelm, confidence, frustration, boundaries, and so on. The coach might respond to the big client download simply with this: "You have brought several important topics forward. Which is most important for us to explore today?" Or, as in the earlier case, "You've brought up a really big topic, but I feel like there's something deeply rooted under it. What is important for us to explore?" In this example, the coach is demonstrating that they have heard the client by using their words, and the coach is more concisely reflecting back the metaphor, repeating the owned words to them, with an invitation to the client to determine what is important and what they want to explore, through what they shared.

Again, I liken coaching to listening to trees falling in a forest. If no one is there to hear the tree fall, did it make a sound? When my client talked about being deeply rooted, did she hear that as important to her sense of place and grounding? Probably not. It's an example of the client's unconscious conceptualization. Again, metaphors are often unconsciously said, but "deeply rooted" is her language, which is instrumental in how the client sees herself. If the coach doesn't hear that tree fall, what opportunity for exploration is missed?

In a study on memory, Penn State psychologists explored attribute amnesia and, along the way, discovered that the memory is selective: "It is commonly believed that you will remember specific details about the things you're attending to, but our experiments show that this is not necessarily true," said Brad Wyble, assistant professor of psychology. "We found that in some cases, people have trouble remembering even very simple pieces of information when they do not expect to have to remember them. Memory is sort of like a camcorder; if you don't hit the 'record' button on the camcorder, it's not going to 'remember' what the lens is pointed at'" (Chen and Wyble 2016, 226).

This research fits with trees falling in a forest. If the client says something important or insightful, they may only remember saying it if the coach supports them, pressing "record" by noticing it and being curious. With metaphors, clients are primed from their own minds to remember the metaphor if the coach, with curiosity, anchors awareness.

I had a client, an executive at Boeing, who was considering getting his team to look at each customer uniquely. As he was talking, he began using the idea of ingredients. I asked how his team determined the ingredients for each customer. That turned on a light bulb in his brain, and he excitedly started talking about his team, thinking about the casserole that each client might need. Different ingredients went into the different casseroles, and they could create a unique recipe for each client. Six months later, he still used the metaphor of the unique casserole and recipe with his team. If I hadn't caught on to the "ingredients" and asked about them, the metaphor would have been just another tree falling that no one had heard.

A Caveat to Using Metaphors

People with atypical neurology, such as those on the autism spectrum or with brain injuries, may be fixated on linear thinking and find the abstractions of metaphor confusing. There has been some research on the use of metaphors in people with atypical brain processing, such as autism or aphasia. This research has generally found that people with atypical brain processing may have difficulty understanding and using metaphors in language due to differences in their cognitive and linguistic abilities.

One study that investigated the use of metaphors in people with autism found that, although they could understand and generate basic metaphors, they had difficulty understanding more complex or abstract ones (Baron-Cohen et al. 2001).

Another study found that people with aphasia, a language disorder that affects the production and comprehension of language, had difficulty understanding and producing metaphors, but this difficulty was related to the complexity of the metaphor rather than to their overall language abilities (Prutting and Kirchner 1987).

In my practical experience, I have worked with clients on the autism spectrum and found that many have no problems using or working with metaphors. But if a person is very literal in their thinking, metaphors may not be the best way for them to explore. The point is not for coaches to make the client use metaphors but to follow the metaphors the client brings to them. If the client brings simple metaphors, stick with those.

There is no need to change or improve the metaphors your clients share. Doing so will likely take the client out of their understanding of their meaning and move them into trying to make sense of your meaning. Remember, the metaphors are theirs to own as they light up their brain.

LEGO Serious Play

LEGO Serious Play (LSP) is an interactive and innovative approach designed to stimulate innovative thinking and improve individual and group performance. LSP employs LEGO bricks to help individuals and groups communicate more deeply. It is grounded in the philosophy of hands-on learning and that everyone should be able to contribute to conversations, decisions, and outcomes.

I took LSP training in 2023 to explore metaphorical and visual communication through a different lens. I mention it in this chapter as a way to explore visual constructs of complex ideas with people on the spectrum who don't do well with the language element of metaphors. It works well with anyone, but for those with language comprehension issues, it becomes a tangible way to explore complex ideas.

With LSP, clients are introduced to a context or challenge. This context could be the exploration of self-awareness, focusing on how understanding oneself better can contribute to personal and professional development. The LEGO set comes with a LEGO mini-person (a mini-me) and a bunch of random bricks. When working with a client, we might spend five minutes and have the client build what is showing up as important today. Clients are invited to construct a physical representation or an artifact of their self-concept with LEGO bricks; this initiates the journey of self-discovery. This active, hands-on approach combines cognitive engagement with tactile learning, which is often underused in adult environments. Through this exercise, the client creates a personal model of themselves, a mini-me, using the bricks, head, legs, and arms. Then they are able to place their mini-me into scenarios that illustrate their thoughts, ideas, feelings, or perceptions. These artifacts have deeply individual meaning for each builder.

The artifacts built from LEGO bricks are far from random;

they serve as metaphors for complex and abstract ideas. People can look at one brick, and it can represent anything. For example, I held a red brick in my mini-me hands, and the red brick represented a heart. That said, the red brick could have represented anything. I had a rabbit on my mini-me head, and it represented bringing in playful thinking. Each person will make meaning from the imagery they create from the LEGOs. It's genius.

It's incredible how each brick, color, or formation a client chooses can signify distinct elements such as emotions, traits, experiences, or values. As such, the model lets clients articulate and visualize their internal states or abstract concepts. This constructionist approach provides clients with a visual language to express their thoughts and emotions, thus deepening their self-awareness. Once individual models are complete, the coach can invite the client to share its meaning. This then becomes the metaphorical representation of their model. This lets individuals reflect on their self-concept and explore it further, deepening understanding. It also opens a window for others to appreciate different perspectives and foster empathy.

Questions

- Reflecting on this chapter, can you identify any owned metaphors that stood out to you? How do these metaphors provide insights into the client's inner experiences?

- How can the use of artful reflection with owned metaphors enhance the coaching process?

- How do you anchor awareness in your coaching conversation and listen for the falling trees?

- How can coaches adapt their approach when working with clients struggling with metaphors?

- Reflecting on the LEGO Serious Play method and its use of tangible artifacts to visualize complex ideas, how has this process enhanced your understanding of metaphors, especially considering those who may struggle with the language element of metaphors?

● What is your biggest takeaway from this chapter?

Reading Recommendation

The LSP Method: How to Engage People and Spark Insights Using the LEGO® Serious Play® Method by Michael Fearne

Chapter 4: Client-Led & Client-Centered

" This process of the good life is not, I am convinced,
a life for the faint-hearted.

—Carl Rogers

As we continue to explore the theory inherent in coaching with metaphors, let's turn toward the idea of partnership. In this chapter, we will discuss the value of coaches allowing themselves to be led by their clients. The idea of partnership is about giving the client agency and the coach following the client's lead. Ultimately, we are talking about the difference between advising and coaching—where the coach steps back and lets the client determine direction and importance. This concept is about tuning into the client's metaphors, the pictures they paint with their words, and letting them guide the conversation.

Think of it as a dance between two partners. The coach is there to provide the space, encouragement, and curiosity, but the client is the one who sets the pace and leads the way. By listening to their client's metaphors, the coach can gain a deeper understanding of their experience, their thoughts and feelings, and the meaning they are making of it all.

What's behind this client-led approach to coaching? That's what we'll be exploring in this chapter by delving into the theoretical foundations of such coaching in order to understand the why of learning to listen and partner more fully with your clients.

Understanding Client-Led Coaching from a Client-Centered Framework

In 2018, a groundbreaking study was conducted to uncover the benefits of client-led conversations. The study showed that when clients are given the reins to lead the conversation, they arrive at more meaningful and practical solutions to their problems (Panayotov and Strahilov 2019). This empowered approach allows clients to take an active role in their healing process and equips them with the tools they need to easily handle future difficulties.

As I delved into this research, I was reminded of Carl Rogers, the renowned psychologist who is considered the father of client-centered therapy. Rogers believed that the relationship between the therapist and the client was critical in facilitating change and personal growth. He emphasized the importance of therapists being genuine, accepting, and empathetic, creating a safe and nonjudgmental space for clients to express themselves. It's fascinating to see how Rogers's nineteen propositions and his theory of a good life align with the principles of client-led coaching. With the results of the study by Panayotov and Strahilov (2019) pointing toward the effectiveness of client-led conversations, it's clear that Rogers was on to something.

In the words of Rogers himself, "The process of the good life is not, I am convinced, a life for the faint-hearted. It involves the stretching and growing of becoming more and more of one's potentialities. It involves the courage to be. It means launching oneself fully into the stream of life."

Rogerian Humanist, Client-Centered Theory

To summarize Rogers's nineteen propositions and his theory in general, he believed that people live in an ever-changing world of experiences and that each of us is the central character in our story. We all want to actualize and ultimately have a good life. From this premise, given that I am the central character in my story and you are the central character in your story, how can my character in my story determine what your character needs or must do to have what you believe to be a good life in your story?

Client-centeredness allows the client to lead me, the coach, through their story; thus, the client directs the coach in exploring their external and internal landscape. This approach is crucial to working with a person's perception framework and exploring how they make meaning. It also takes skill to learn to be curious on behalf of another person. But in understanding and then using the clients' framework and language, we can more fully partner with our clients and create a safe space within which the clients' internal landscape is more fully explored.

People react to the experiences they perceive, and in this perceptual experience, they create their reality. Essentially, what the client is aware of is the reality for them. It is critical to understand that everybody lives in a constantly changing world where they are at the center, and the continually changing world around them becomes their reality.

As people navigate reality, they react and respond to their perception of their experiences. Simply said, what you say, think, and do comes from your perception of the reality in which you live. Along with this perception of reality you hold is an externalization of reality that it is happening "out there" rather than that you are experiencing your reality "in here."

People have a fundamental tendency and desire to grow into their best selves. This idea of self-actualization made Rogers pivotal; instead of human beings who just existed, he believed that people wanted to become the best version of themselves. Not all people fall into this category, but the majority of those you come across as a coach want to be better human beings. The theory maintains that human beings have a fundamental desire to actualize and enhance their experiences, as well as themselves.

Rogers believed that the best place to understand human behavior is from the internal frame of reference of the individual person. If we're looking at this from a coaching viewpoint, we need to be cognizant that the best place for a human being to actualize—or, in my language, to find an empowered agency—comes from within themselves. This self-exploration takes courage. It means that we need to find ways to make the investigation safe. We need to learn to be curious about the clients' external experience by exploring it from an internal inquiry framework.

Employing a Socratic style, you use inquiry not to lead your client to a specific outcome but to explore awareness so that they can discover the most meaningful outcome. This supports the client's agency to choose the actions and results they want in their best life.

Emotions become doorways to curiosity. When we think about emotions in a conversation, emotions express how the person is experiencing themselves within their reality. This is a place for curiosity because behaviors come from the person's relationship to their perceived reality.

Gestalt Coaching

Another theory that supports the client-centered approach is Gestalt coaching. In a conversation with Dorothy Siminovitch, PhD, MCC, she stated, "In Gestalt coaching, there is the idea that who we are, our presence, as coach, really meets biologically with you, your presence as client. So the meeting between me and you is understood as relational. We are meeting from a point of view of who am I being, and what's my presence. And how do I see you collaboratively and respond?" (Dorothy Siminovitch, pers. comm., February 2023).

Gestalt coaching is about the client's present experience of their situation. There is always the understanding that our client is the guide in the work. How collaborative are we in the role of coach? It's a constant thing that you need to keep top of mind: Are you speaking from your "I" to the client as a "you"? Or is the conversation peer to peer, the client and the coach creating together?

Again, the understanding within this theory is the idea of self-exploration and insight. By that very nature, the client has to lead. The client is not just an equal, and the partnership is relational with the client as the one who is guiding the coach. It is the client's self-exploration and awareness that are important.

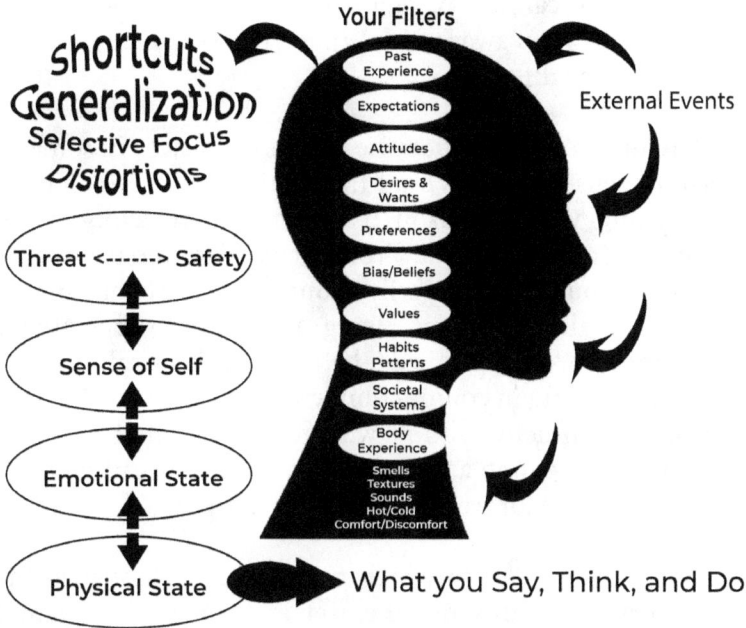

Discovering the "I" Within

Who are we really? Our sense of self is shaped by the events happening around us and how we process them. Our past experiences, beliefs, values, habits, and even physical sensations all play a role in how we perceive the world and react to it.

Our sense of self, or "I," develops as external events move through our filtration system of experiences, expectations, attitudes, desires, preferences, beliefs, biases, values, habits, the systems that we operate within, and even our internal physical responses (embodied experience) to situations, such as feeling hot or cold, or noticing how we are breathing, or being aware of our heart rate.

The result of the external event is that we perceive it as either positive or negative. We experience it on a spectrum from safety to threat. Due to the safety/threat spectrum, we develop an emotional response. Emotions accompany behavior directed toward a goal. Emotions are related to the perceived significance created uniquely by each person. We cannot make assumptions; we must ask questions to evoke individual awareness. What triggers my fear and what triggers yours will be different.

Behaviors are adopted because they're consistent in some way with a person's sense of self. We see this all the time. Human beings do not do anything without reason. If somebody is behaving in a certain way, there is a reason for it. From a coaching perspective, you must be curious—but not necessarily about where the behavior came from; that is the realm of therapy. Being curious and supporting the client to become aware of a particular behavior and to explore whether it is or is not working in conjunction with what they say they want as a goal is part of self-actualization, whatever that might be for them. Behaviors do not happen in a vacuum; they happen because the person believed that behavior was helpful at some point.

There are instances in which individuals do not own their behavior. Instead, they distance themselves from it. For example, someone who micromanages others might not see themselves as controlling: "I just want things done correctly." Through the lack of recognition of the behavior, it is disowned and paradoxically still continues.

This disowning means that human beings create adjustments to their sense of self. They take in their experiences and assimilate them to become consistent with that sense of self. If people see themselves as good, they may rationalize their behavior. Of course, we live in our own heads, so we understand why we do what we do. Micromanaging is translated into helping. We give ourselves grace around this behavior. Often, this same grace isn't given to others.

Difficulties within a person's experience exist due to denied awareness of the significance of these experiences, which are consequently not integrated into their sense of self. When the situation exists, there's a potential for tension and discomfort. We are out of alignment with something core inside us.

Any experience that is inconsistent with a person's sense of self may be perceived as a threat. When we perceive things as a threat, we often feel internally pressured to make things (externally) different to protect ourselves (internally). When we feel threatened, our capacity for creativity and curiosity is diminished.

My Aha Moment

Many years ago, when I was in college, I was a volunteer hospital advocate for a rape crisis center. My role was to go to the hospital and advocate for someone who had just experienced having all their power taken from them. One element of the training I received was that my job, first and foremost, was to return power to that person. I would tell them, "Hello, my name is Lyssa. I am an advocate for you. I can stay with you, sit outside your door, call people on your behalf; I can hold your hand or not; I am here for you in any way you need. I will wait, and if you change your mind or need me to support you in some other way, guide me. I am here for you."

My aha moment was realizing that personal agency is often the thing people feel the least. You don't have to experience a major trauma to feel like you have had your power stripped away. Working for a bad boss in a soul-sucking job or not prioritizing your value— really, any number of things—can leave you disempowered. In this, client-led coaching is key to giving people their power back.

Partnering in Coaching

In coaching, client-centered strategies create a dynamic partnership that's tailored to each individual's unique perspective and objectives. This collaborative approach fosters a safe, nonjudgmental space where both coach and client can explore the client's experiences with an attitude of open curiosity. Metaphors bridge this partnership, inviting a deeper self-awareness and a richer understanding of personal growth possibilities. Using metaphors to navigate this exploratory process encourages the client to reframe and expand their worldview, offering new avenues for understanding and personal evolution.

In a client-centered coaching approach, the focus is squarely on the individual's unique needs and experiences. The goal is to help clients attain deeper self-awareness, self-acceptance, and personal growth. This is achieved in a secure environment that encourages exploration without threatening the person's sense of self. The approach relies on open curiosity as a tool for examining experiences, allowing clients the freedom to reframe and expand their understanding of their own lives.

When people integrate and accept all their experiences into their sense of self, without fear, they become whole. And from this sense of wholeness, they become more accepting of others. As people accept themselves and their experiences, they can rewrite their narratives to include updated information concerning their value systems, distortions, and biases. They can explore those internal concepts and become self-aware/self-actualized and thus more open and resilient to change.

Both Rogerian and Gestalt coaching illuminate how these client-centered paradigms empower individuals and enhance their sense of agency. As a coach, tuning into your clients' metaphors enriches your understanding of their inner world and elevates the coaching partnership. That's why diving deep into the theoretical underpinnings of client-led coaching is invaluable for truly grasping the transformative power of collaborative exploration.

Questions

- Reflecting on this chapter, how can client-led coaching enhance the coaching process? What are the potential benefits of letting the client lead the conversation?

- How can integrating Rogerian and Gestalt coaching approaches support client empowerment and agency?

- How might metaphors support you in partnering with your clients' internal landscape?

- What will you play with in your coaching?

Reading Recommendation

A Gestalt Coaching Primer: The Path toward Awareness Intelligence by Dorothy Siminovitch

CHAPTER 5: POSITIVE EMOTIONAL ATTRACTION

" We know that giving someone ideas as to what they "should" do and how they "should" change, to be more effective, often has the opposite effect.

—Richard Boyatzis, *Helping People Change*

The idea of unconditional positive regard and client-centered coaching is aligned with the idea of coaching with compassion, which is explored in the work of Richard Boyatzis and Anthony Jack at Case Western Reserve University. Their research on positive emotional attraction (PEA) and negative emotional attraction (NEA) demonstrates how subtle shifts in a person's feeling of threat/judgment or safety/acceptance impact the experience of working with a coach. Even with very nice coaches, due to NEA, the sense of being told to do something or being pointed in the direction of a perceived failure leaves the client feeling judged.

Anything that triggers judgment will shut the brain down to creativity and openness. Think fight, flight, freeze, and freak out. In a nutshell, coaching with compassion, free from judgment and filled with positive regard, illuminates the path to unlocking the client's full potential as their minds light up. As coaches, that's what we want to happen.

PEA and NEA

A study with twenty-three undergraduate students examined how the brain activated based on the students' snippets of PEA and NEA conversations with coaches (Jack et al. 2013). Each participant received two sorts of coaching: One type focused on a personal vision of what the person wanted for their future, and the other more focused on the challenges. What was getting in the way? What did they face in order to meet expectations?

After the participants experienced each coaching style, they went through a series of questionnaires and interviews, as well as having their brains recorded by functional magnetic resonance imaging (fMRI). As the participants listened to clips from their coaching sessions, the fMRIs showed where their brains lit up.

The researchers found that the participants appreciated the coaches' time and felt that they benefited from the coaching. That's what we often see—clients get something, even from performance-based coaching. Yet with the coaching based on PEA, they noticed in the fMRIs that there was a greater engagement in the brain areas associated with motivation. The patterns of brain activation as captured by the fMRI showed a significant increase in activity in brain regions involved in perceptual imagery in individuals who had received PEA coaching rather than NEA.

With PEA coaching, people were more likely to perceive themselves in a more empowered way. They had better capacity to open up to ideas; to see things in new, creative ways; and to see more possibilities. They also felt that the coaching was much more inspirational, and there was a higher degree of trust and safety in the PEA setting.

Conversely, in NEA, coaching was perceived to be more judgmental, and the researchers saw more significant activity in brain regions associated with the sympathetic stress response. The regions that were activated were related to stress—feeling self-conscious, engaging in self-judgment, and feeling judged by external forces, which, of course, did not lead to the client experiencing the same level of motivation. Instead, the NEA coaching instigated more negative emotions in the client. Feeling judged creates a pressure of obligation: "You need to do something different." This leads to other negative emotions, such as shame.

Shame is triggered when people feel judged negatively. This was explored in the work of John Bradshaw (1988) and has been continued by Brené Brown (2015). People already have an internal narrative about themselves that tends toward the negative. If anybody—a friend, a parent, a therapist, a coach, a mentor, or an adviser—triggers that sense of shame, the person's capacity to take in information is limited or quickly hits critical mass. People react in a myriad of ways: shutting down, getting angry or defensive, or spiraling into even more negative self-judgment.

Going back to the research by Panayotov and Strahilov (2019) that was discussed in the previous chapter, shifting to client-led conversations has the benefit of empowering clients to find solutions to their problems, solving other problems of client/therapist misunderstandings, supporting clients to find solutions to their current dilemmas, and prepares them for handling future difficulties. Because effective therapy and coaching are based on asking useful questions, the more capable clients become, the less therapy they will need in the future.

A brain that feels judged interprets it as a threat. A brain that feels threatened on any level, even an existential threat, will switch to survival mode. The perception of a threat can be so powerful and the need to survive so strong that the mind can no longer absorb more information. People become reactive and cannot be curious, open-minded, or find humor in that state. Clients rarely lead themselves into these darker places if the coach's questions are useful in exploring safely below the waterline and have a client-determined outcome for the conversation.

Most of us have had that experience where we felt like we were drinking from a fire hose. It's just too much information, and we're overwhelmed by it. For a person to change the way they see themselves within an experience, they will need to have an absence of the perception of threat. The client leading the coach means that the client decides how much, how far, and how to explore the often tender places that need to be investigated so that they can either learn from them or let them go.

The humanistic or Gestalt framework reduces shame and supports a person's empowered agency. We are not getting into the weeds of what went wrong but rather what the person wants to learn or let go of so that we move forward. It's helpful for coaches to understand that their clients ultimately want purpose and a drive toward wholeness and self-actualization—that is, a good life. The journey requires courage from the client and the coach to bravely peek into hidden spaces and explore new, more useful meanings.

How Metaphors Connect to Client-Centered Coaching

You may be asking yourself, *"But Lyssa, why are we talking about this? I came here for metaphors."* Understanding the client-centered framework and the neuroscience of PEA allows you to show up with your clients in ways that reduce defensiveness or a sense of judgment so that they become more open to growing from their experiences. Learning to listen to the metaphors that clients share with us means partnering in a client-led conversation. Metaphorically speaking, we must learn to take our hands off the wheel and give the wheel to the person who owns the car.

By listening deeply and tuning your ears to the metaphors your client shares, you will find it very difficult to trigger negative judgment or shame. You are using your clients' visual language—the image schemas that their brain has created. This is what it is to partner fully.

"Client-led" means that I believe that only the client can decide what is important to explore and how they want to explore what they believe is important. It's the clients work to do, so as coaches, we ask, "What do you want or need to learn from this experience? What do you need to name or acknowledge to move forward? What might we explore so that you can move toward your goals?" Because these questions require courage, metaphors can give a bit of distance and reduce the negative self-judgment that slows the process. Through metaphors, the client can develop the capacity to be introspective, allowing them to be experimental, bold, brave, and adaptable in an ever-changing world. The goal is to find ways to hold the space of both vision and action. Yet the actions themselves must come from the client.

In coaching, we hold an outlook that the client is whole, capable, resourceful, and creative. And if this is true—and I believe it is—then wisdom is within the client. If the deepest coaching goal is to self-actualize, then clients will recognize their inherent expertise and agency over their sense of self. The coach is invited to learn to trust the client and to let themselves be led through the client's internal landscape. It's a place the client may have yet to venture into on their own.

Questions

- How does coaching with compassion, free from judgment and filled with positive regard, impact the client's experience and brain activation?

- How does the perception of judgment and threat impact the brain's ability to absorb information and engage in creative thinking?

- How can metaphors play a role in creating a safe and nonjudgmental space for clients to explore their experiences and make meaning of them?

- From this chapter, what are you considering playing with in your coaching conversations.

Reading Recommendation

"*Coaching with Compassion Can 'Light Up' Human Thoughts,*" by Case Western Reserve University

Chapter 6: Enhancing Understanding & Memory

> " Because thinking is hard, conditions have to be right for this
> curiosity to thrive, or we quit thinking...
> People are naturally curious, but curiosity is fragile.
>
> —Daniel Willingham, *Why Don't Students Like School?*

If you have ever found yourself in a coaching conversation and are completely lost—maybe the client is bringing forward one thousand ideas and they all seem disconnected—you may be experiencing cognitive load. The same is probably happening to your client as they whirl and spin, trying to explain some complex situation, idea or feeling they are experiencing. This is where many coaches get hooked into the need to understand.

I am going to argue that the coach doesn't actually need to understand the situation; instead, they need to notice the client's confusion, let go of needing to know, recognize that the client is also probably confused, and then work to hold the space for the client to explore the confusion so that they can gain clarity. Creative thinking is the desire to reconcile the novel with the known, which can be difficult at times. Metaphors are a passageway through the inherent confusion of understanding and communicating complex ideas.

"When you solve a problem or satisfy your curiosity, your brain may reward itself with a small burst of a naturally occurring chemical in the brain's pleasure system. Even though the neurochemistry is not completely understood, it seems undeniable that people take pleasure in solving problems," observes Daniel T. Willingham in Why Don't Students Like School? A Cognitive Scientist Answers Questions about How the Mind Works and What It Means for the Classroom. This concept applies as much to coaching as it does to teaching. It serves as a reminder that to illuminate our clients' minds, we should facilitate their problem-solving process. Willingham further writes, "It's notable, too, that the pleasure is in solving the problem. Working on a problem without any sense of making progress is not pleasurable."

Such insights underscore the importance of asking thought-provoking questions, fostering awareness, and refraining from providing immediate answers, thus stimulating curiosity and deeper understanding in our clients. It also suggests that dwelling on unsolvable issues may lead to frustration and stifle curiosity. The premise that curiosity is a thirst for understanding reinforces the belief that the role of a coach or teacher is not to provide solutions, but to cultivate an environment where clients or students can be curious, explore their thoughts, and reach their own insights.

Cognitive Load Theory

Cognitive load theory (CLT) is a concept that originated from the field of educational psychology, largely established by John Sweller in 1988. The theory examines the amount of mental effort, or load, an individual's cognitive system undergoes while processing information.

The foundation of CLT is built upon our understanding that human cognitive architecture includes a working memory, where new information is first processed, and a long-term memory, where it is stored. The capacity of working memory is extremely limited, and it is highly susceptible to overload.

In the book Efficiency in Learning: Evidence-Based Guidelines to Manage Cognitive Load (2006), Sweller, Ruth Colvin Clark, and Frank Nguyen explain that CLT describes methods to optimize the use of limited working memory resources during learning. The authors categorize cognitive load into three types:

1. *Intrinsic load*: This relates to the inherent difficulty of the content being taught or shared. Complex topics with multiple interacting elements have a higher intrinsic load.

2. *Extraneous load*: This refers to the manner in which information is presented to learners. If it is presented in a complex or confusing way, the extraneous load is increased.

3. *Germane load*: This refers to the cognitive resources used to process and understand information. It's associated with the construction of schemas (a pattern of thought or behavior that organizes categories of information and the relationships among them) in long-term memory.

Jan Plass and colleagues (2010) further elaborate on how these different types of cognitive load can affect a person's ability to learn new information. They highlight that effective instructional design seeks to minimize extraneous cognitive load, manage intrinsic cognitive load, and maximize germane cognitive load. This balance enables efficient learning by preventing the overloading of working memory and promoting the formation of effective schemas in long-term memory.

CLT and metaphors in coaching are intimately intertwined concepts that contribute to effective learning and understanding.

Drawing on Sweller's work, we know that the human cognitive system can be easily overwhelmed by complex information, causing learning to become challenging. As bridges between language and mental imagery, metaphors can help alleviate this issue by reducing the intrinsic cognitive load—the inherent complexity of important conceptual information with which the client is wrestling.

When we use metaphors, we convert abstract or complex concepts into something more relatable and easier to visualize, thus reducing the intrinsic cognitive load. This ties in with the conceptual metaphor concept, as the same brain areas for processing visual information also process metaphors.

Take, for example, a coaching session focused on a client's desire to explore and make strategic business decisions. The concept can be quite intricate and abstract. However, consider a client who uses a metaphor such as this: "I feel like I am on a chessboard, and sometimes I am a pawn, and other times I feel like the king, only able to make one step in any direction. I need a way to use the whole board." As a coach hears this, they have a deeper understanding of the complexity of the topic, and by exploring the chessboard, the complex decision-making is made significantly easier to comprehend. The coach can invite the client to talk about what other chess pieces they might like to embody. What do those pieces mean to the client? What shift needs to happen that would allow, say, the knight to come forward? This use of the metaphor simplifies the information by connecting it to a known concept (chess pieces/chessboard), lessening the intrinsic cognitive load.

Simultaneously, this can also increase the germane load, the part of the cognitive load devoted to processing and constructing new schemas. The metaphor acts as an aid to help connect new information to existing knowledge (chess strategies/business strategies), facilitating the development of a new schema or, in layman's terms, a new story about how the client might look at the situation from different vantage points and ultimately create new ways to make strategic business decisions.

By minimizing extraneous cognitive load, the unnecessary cognitive load is generated by an exhaustive explanation of the situation, which happens when the coach asks the client to explain the situation. This also happens if the coach interjects their own complex or irrelevant metaphors; they can here again increase the extraneous load. We can, instead, stay in the flow of the client's metaphor/thinking and optimize insight, awareness, and learning. However, when the client brings the simple metaphors forward, just like the one about chess in our example, it can help keep the extraneous load to a minimum.

I see CLT and the use of conceptual metaphors in coaching as intimately intertwined concepts that contribute to effective learning and understanding. As we have most likely experienced in our own lives and in coaching sessions, we know that the human cognitive system can be easily overwhelmed by complex information, causing learning to become challenging. Metaphors, as bridges between language and mental imagery, can help alleviate this issue by reducing the intrinsic cognitive load and the inherent complexity of new information that the client is processing.

Dual Coding Theory

Dual coding theory (DCT) is another cognitive theory that argues that human cognition involves the activity of two distinct cognitive systems, verbal and nonverbal, that can operate independently and also interact with each other. Allan Paivio introduced this theory in the late 1960s and early 1970s.

According to Paivio's seminal work, *Mental Representations: A Dual Coding Approach* (1986), the verbal system deals with linguistic information, such as spoken or written language, while the nonverbal system deals with nonlinguistic information, including images, sounds (that are not words), and physical sensations.

The fundamental assumption of DCT is that we understand and remember information better if it is presented to us in both verbal and visual formats. In other words, our brain can remember images and words independently, but combining both can enhance memory and understanding.

Later research, including a study by Paivio and James Clark (1991), explores the implications of this theory for education. The authors argued that materials combining words and appropriate visuals are generally more understandable and memorable than materials that use words alone.

This theory is supported by numerous studies, such as one by Marc Marschark and R. Reed Hunt (1989), which showed that memory recall was significantly better when information was presented with both words and related pictures compared with words or pictures alone. I remember taking a Spanish course where the word for tree is árbol. I was told to think of a ball that was up in a tree. I have never forgotten that.

In practical terms, DCT implies that teaching strategies should ideally incorporate both verbal and visual information to support learning and comprehension. This also fits into coaching from the perspective that if a client uses a powerful metaphor, and the coach and the client explore the complexities through the lens of that metaphor, the client has more access to remembering the insights they create. They don't forget as easily the learning and meaning they made.

For Your Consideration

In summary, the effective use of CLT and DCT in coaching can transform what might be a whirlwind of confusion into a pathway of clarity. Recognizing the cognitive load we and our clients experience when grappling with complex ideas and emotions can help coaches facilitate more insightful and productive conversations.

The use of metaphors, especially conceptual ones, emerges as a potent tool in this process. As bridges between verbal language and visual imagery, metaphors can simplify complex ideas, reduce cognitive load, and engage both verbal and visual processing pathways.

When your clients use metaphors, such as "having a full plate," they make their experiences more tangible and create an environment conducive to better recall and understanding, thanks to DCT. As coaches, rather than aiming to fully understand the intricacies of a client's situation, our role can be to hold space for them to explore their metaphors and make meaning from their experiences. Thus, we can empower them to navigate the confusion, build new narratives/schemas, and emerge with newfound clarity and insights.

Questions

- How can the use of metaphors in coaching help reduce cognitive load and facilitate deeper understanding and clarity for both the coach and the client?

- How do metaphors function as tools in coaching to reduce cognitive load and facilitate understanding of complex ideas?

- In what ways can you leverage the power of metaphors as bridges between language and mental imagery to support your clients in simplifying complex ideas, reducing cognitive load, and fostering deeper insights and transformation?

Reading Recommendation

Why Don't Students Like School? A Cognitive Scientist Answers Questions about How the Mind Works and What It Means for the Classroom by Daniel T. Willingham

Chapter 7: Clean Language & Symbolic Modeling

" Our skill with metaphor, with thought, is one thing —
prodigious and inexplicable; our reflective awareness of that skill
is quite another thing—very incomplete, distorted, fallacious,
over-simplifying.

— Ivor A. Richards, *The Philosophy of Rhetoric*

When first introduced to the concept of clean language, many coaches might grapple with its seeming rigidity, especially if they cherish the art of free-flowing conversation. The initial reaction might be one of resistance, an inner questioning of how such a structured set of questions aligns with the spontaneity of personal coaching. But as one ventures deeper, the important elements of listening are profound. The essence of clean language isn't about confining the dialogue but about channeling it to create a client-led conversation between the coach and the client.

Clean language was developed by David Grove, a New Zealand therapist known for his innovative and effective approaches to helping people overcome challenges and make meaningful changes. At its core, clean language epitomizes the less-is-more paradigm. The technique is not just an exercise in linguistic precision but a journey into minimalism. By diligently holding on to the client's vernacular and refraining from interjecting personal interpretations, it crafts a dialogue that's undeniably client-centered. There's a subtle brilliance to this: Each question, simple and direct, dissolves any preconceived biases, allowing the client's narrative to shine through, pure and unfiltered.

Symbolic Modeling

Symbolic modeling is a coaching and therapy method that uses clean language to help individuals explore their thoughts, feelings, and experiences through their own metaphors and symbols, facilitating deeper understanding and personal change. It was developed by Penny Tompkins and James Lawley, based on Grove's work and his clean language concept.

Symbolic modeling focuses on preserving the logic of the client's language, and often their metaphors, by using their exact words and by asking specific types of questions. These questions can relate to attributes, location, metaphorical comparisons, relationships, sequences, sources, and intentions. This questioning technique aims to avoid contaminating the client's internal landscape and leaving them in the seat of authority regarding meaning. Symbolic modeling stands out because it uses clean language as a tool to help people dive deeply into their thoughts, feelings, and experiences. The goal? To help them understand themselves better and to tackle challenges in a more effective way.

The core of clean language is its focus on the client's own words, especially when it comes to their metaphors. Instead of interpreting or rephrasing, the coach or therapist uses the client's exact language. Grove discovered that by asking people a series of open-ended questions that reflect the words and the metaphors they use, he could help them access their unconscious minds and discover their insights and solutions. He called this method clean language, and it became the foundation of symbolic modeling (Tompkins and Lawley 1997).

Some of the ways symbolic modeling is used today include the following:

- Helping people overcome phobias and other fears

- Improving communication and relationships
- Resolving conflicts and improving teamwork
- Enhancing personal and professional development
- Supporting recovery from trauma or abuse
- Enhancing creativity and problem-solving skills

Symbolic modeling helps clients generate metaphors and symbols using a set of questions developed from clean language principles. "At its core, symbolic modeling is a simple set of questions originally designed to use client metaphors as the entry point for supporting them to have positive changes. It continues to evolve and is now also used to work with conceptual and sensory descriptions" (James Lawley, pers. comm., November 3, 2023).

Clean language and symbolic modeling questions may feel prescriptive, yet they are powerful communication tools that help people deeply and meaningfully explore their thoughts, feelings, and experiences. It's called clean because it's free from preconceived ideas, biases, assumptions, or judgments on the part of the coach. This allows the person being coached to discover their own insights and solutions.

Clean language has a set of twelve questions while symbolic modeling consists mostly of eight basic/classic questions. The coach uses the eight open-ended questions in any order to craft and reflect the words, emotional states, and metaphors used by the person being coached. These questions represent the most universal of the twelve clean language questions (Lawley 2023).

The eight basic symbolic modeling questions are as follows:

- And what would you like to have happen?
- And is there anything else about [. . .]?
- And what kind of [. . .] is that [. . .]?
- And where/whereabouts is [. . .]?

- And that's [. . .] like what?
- And when/as [x], what happens to [y]?
- And what happens just before [event]?
- And what happens next? And then what happens?

Again, these questions are not in a particular order and can be used in any sequence. They are designed to help the client explore their thoughts, feelings, and experiences. The goal is that the questions let clients access their unconscious mind, where their deepest insights and wisdom reside. Ultimately, the client will discover their own insights and solutions by accessing their unconscious mind.

I don't use clean language or symbolic modeling specifically; however, I like the clean, simple partnering that happens when we honor people's words and listen deeply. I am intrigued by people's results when using the process.

Here is a short example of clean language/symbolic modeling in action with Lawley from a 2015 video. I was given permission from him to share a brief snippet to illustrate the process. I have bolded the strong words the client shares and how they appear in the coach's or therapist's powerful questions.

Coach: What would you like to happen?

Client: I would like **to work on stress levels** that **I feel** with our **business** systems **changing.**

Coach: And you'd like to work on the **stress levels that you feel** about your **business changing.** And so, when you'd like to **work on** those **stress levels,** what kind of **levels** are those **levels?**

Client: **They're elevated.**

Coach **They're elevated.** Ah. And is there anything else about the **elevation** of those **levels?**

Client: **They are stronger than I have had in business before.**

Coach: Ah, so they're **elevated levels** that are **stronger** than what **you've had in business before**. And when those **levels of stress are elevated and stronger** than what **you've had in business before**, what would you like to have happen?

Client: **I would like to learn to manage my state.**

Coach: Ah, so you'd like to learn **to manage your state.** And when **you manage your state**, what **kind of manage is that manage?**

Client: **A self-aware and self-healing manage.**

Coach: **A self-aware and self-healing manage.** And is there anything else about being **self-aware and self-healing?**

Client: It's **quick** and it **doesn't require intervention from others.**

Coach: Ah, and **it's quick** and **doesn't require intervention from others.** And when you are **self-aware** like that, where is that **self-aware?**

Client: Err . . . it is **in my heart.**

Coach: And as **you're self-aware in your heart**, that's a **quick self-aware** that **doesn't require intervention from others.** And when **you're self-aware in your heart** like that, **what kind of heart is self-aware like that?**

Client: **A warm and widely aware heart.**

Coach: So it's **warm and widely aware.** Is there anything else about **a heart that's warm and widely aware?**

The bottom line here is that by using the client's language, the coach/therapist is instrumental in the client hearing themselves and making the connection among their ideas, metaphors, and somatic experience and then ultimately hearing their tree fall in the forest.

As the person responds to the questions, the coach listens attentively and follows their lead, using the client's words and metaphors to guide the conversation. This helps the person connect with their internal narrative and emotions and explore them in a safe and supportive environment. By the end of the conversation, the client gets to a warm and widely aware heart connected by cables to others, and they are now in deeply embodied and visual language. This image of a warm heart connected to others is going to stay with the client, and the process has supported the client to explore in a new way what they need to manage their stress.

What a Coach Might Take from Clean Language Principles

The first time I heard the clean language style, it didn't resonate. I like having more conversational flexibility, so this structure isn't how my brain works. Regardless, there is much to learn from clean language: to be more client-led, neutral, and simple; use more concise, open-ended questions; and be in partnership with our clients. From the many coaching assessments that I have done, learning to ask clean, client-led, concise questions benefits both coach and client.

Although it might seem formulaic, the success of clean language and symbolic modeling lies in the less-is-more philosophy. By maintaining the client's language as the basis of inquiry, the coach ensures a client-led, neutral, and empowering conversation. These simple, neutral questions are ones only the client can answer. There is no preconceived solution being formulated by the questioner. In the Lawley example, the coach is not telling the client what they should or shouldn't do to solve the stress. The coach doesn't get in the weeds by asking, "Tell me more about your stress," or "Tell me more about these business changes." The questions are simple and concise, using the clients' language as the basis for the inquiry. This creates greater agency, ownership, and empowerment for the client.

Clean language offers a structured way to explore the client's inner world without imposing the therapist's own interpretations, metaphors, or assumptions. This minimizes the risk of contaminating the client's experience and ensures that the conversational journey stays client-centered (Tompkins et al. 2005).

By focusing on the client's exact words and using a limited set of open-ended questions, clean language helps develop and deepen the client's metaphors for their experiences, feelings, and aspirations. This is especially significant because, as we have learned, metaphors are not just linguistic expressions; they represent deeper cognitive and emotional processes. As clients explore these metaphors, they can often arrive at novel insights, experience emotional breakthroughs, or identify actionable steps. Overall, clean language can enrich the coaching or therapeutic process by delving deeply into a client's subjective experience, opening doors to greater self-understanding and change.

The neutral and open-ended partnership principles fit very nicely with the ICF competencies. As an ICF assessor, I have discovered that clean, simple questions often meet many more of the competencies than long, confusing, or coach-directed questions. In my work, I am on a learning journey toward clean, simple, and client-led questions because they encourage empowered partnership and work better with the client's mental flow and reduction of cognitive load.

Why Does This Matter?

Clean language and symbolic modeling matter greatly. Both show a path that respects the client's perspective, and it prevents the coach from introducing their own biases or interpretations. "Clean Language inhibits the coach's natural desire to suggest ways to fix, heal, or resolve the client's problems" (James Lawley, pers. comm., November 3, 2023).

By sticking closely to the client's words and metaphors, the coach ensures that any insights or realizations come directly from the client. The client remains in control of the meaning and interpretation of their experiences, which can lead to more genuine and lasting change. Let's remind ourselves of Rogers and the client-led approach; there is an important connectedness to the ideas of clean language. Using the client's language and metaphors empowers the client to be the expert on their life and experiences. The primary goal in coaching is to create an environment where clients feel seen, heard, understood, and empowered to find their own solutions. In this way, clean language and symbolic modeling have much to offer coaches as a way of holding space for transformational conversations.

Questions

- As you reflect on this chapter, what part of clean language and/ or symbolic modeling might benefit your coaching?

- How can clean language and symbolic modeling principles, including neutrality, simplicity, and open-endedness, support greater client agency, ownership, and empowerment in the coaching process?

- What is an important takeaway from this chapter?

Recommended Reading

Clean Language: Revealing Metaphors and Opening Minds by Wendy Sullivan and Judy Rees

Chapter 8: Embodied Experience

" Embodiment means we no longer say, I had this experience;
we say, I am this experience.

—Sue Monk Kidd, *The Dance of the Dissident Daughter*

The embodied mind is a Buddhist philosophy that thoughts are connected to the whole body. It's been studied through the lens of neuroscience. The senses are explored through three primary categories: exteroception, proprioception, and interoception. We will examine each of these and how they go beyond the primary five senses we have already discussed: sight, smell, hearing, taste, and touch.

Embodied cognition suggests that your mind is not a separate entity from your body but rather that your body and the environment play an important role in shaping your cognitive processes. According to this theory, the way you think and understand the world is not just the result of mental processes that happen inside your head but also is influenced by the physical interactions you have with the world around you.

One of the key ideas behind embodied cognition is that our cognitive processes are shaped by the way we perceive and interact with the world through our senses and movements. Holding heavy items feels heavy; holding light items feels light. When you talk about having a heavy heart, you've embodied the perception of heavy in a new domain.

Embodiment is about how your thinking is connected to your experiences outside and inside your body. Your body experiences come from a multisensory perspective of inhabiting space inside and outside yourself. Simply stated, your ability to experience and sense the world around you is much more expansive than the five senses would have you believe. The mind and the body are deeply interconnected, and your cognitive processes are shaped by the physical interactions you are having within yourself and the world around you.

Let's delve into the categories through which our perceptions are studied and understood (Kandel et al. 2013).

Perception

Embarking on sensory exploration is akin to becoming an astute observer of a hidden inner universe. It's a realm where your senses intertwine to paint vivid pictures of the external world while keeping a pulse on the undercurrents of your inner experiences. Your senses guide you through the landscapes of perception to the heart of how you engage with the many aspects of your environment and your inner world.

- *Exteroception:* This acts as your personal interface with the external world, allowing you to experience the sound of a crackling fire, the aroma of a sumptuous meal, or the cacophony of city life. It's the sentinel that alerts you to the experience of stimuli beyond the confines of your skin.

- *Proprioception:* This is your body's internal GPS. It equips you with an innate sense of spatial awareness, orienting you within the jostle of a crowd or the serenity of a sprawling meadow. Proprioception is the invisible choreographer of your movements, the internal sense that guides you through the spatial elements of living in a three-dimensional world.

- *Interoception:* This is how you attune to the signals that resonate within your body. It's the quiet conversation between body and mind governing your inner workings, things like heart rate, hunger, and tension. On a basic level, it tells you when you're hungry or tired. On a deeper level, it can clue you into emotional needs, like a hunger for learning. The better you listen to these internal cues, the better you'll understand what your body is saying to you.

Mind, Body, Memory, and Behavior

When you have a felt-body experience, you tend to remember it. Remembering the sensation of riding on a roller coaster, sipping a delicious warm drink, tasting a lemon, or stubbing your toe doesn't take much effort. Those experiences live inside you forever; you can easily take yourself back to that moment whenever you want.

If you explore experiences and emotions through the somatic lens, you know what calm feels like in your body, not just in your head. If I ask you to tell me what calm is for you, you can recall how you experience it. As I write this, my calm feels steady and balanced. I have a soft belly and am open to new ideas and can focus my attention. I can contrast this to when I experience excitement: My mind is zipping one hundred miles an hour, and I am bouncing from one idea to another. This awareness supports me in being curious about my experience and what it has to tell me and in considering what state I need to embody to continue writing these words.

Narayanan Kandasamy and colleagues (2016) examined the differences between successful and less successful traders on the London Stock Exchange. The question the researchers were exploring was about interoception. "Interoception is the sensing of physiological signals originating inside the body, such as hunger, pain, and heart rate. People with greater sensitivity to interoceptive signals, as measured by, for example, tests of heartbeat detection, perform better in laboratory studies of risky decision-making. However, there has been little field work to determine if interoceptive sensitivity contributes to success in real-world, high-stakes risk taking" (Kandasamy et al. 2016).

In a nutshell, what they discovered was that traders who were better able to feel their heartbeat tended to be more successful.

Evidence suggests that interoceptive sensitivity contributes "to profitable risk taking in the financial markets" (Kandasamy et al. 2016). The better the traders were at reading the messages from their bodies, the more successful they were. Interoception was not just managing their heart rate; the interoceptive awareness was also giving them valuable information. And when they used that information, they tended to have better results.

Something for coaches to consider is how well you notice your own physical experience, your heart rate. The more you can, the more likely you are to use it to inform your curiosity for the sorts of questions you ask your clients: "As you shared that experience, I noticed a sense of calm, or excitement, or a tightening in my chest. What are you noticing for yourself?" Like the traders in London, coaches who have access to their own experience and can share it in an open and unattached manner have the potential to be more successful at partnering with their clients.

Metaphors and Embodiment

One constant is that we understand abstract concepts through metaphorical idea containers. Metaphors are mental shortcuts that compare abstract ideas to concrete things we can experience. For example, when we say, "I'm grasping an idea," we're using a metaphor that connects the abstract concept of understanding to the concrete action of physically grasping something. This suggests that our brains use these metaphors to make sense of abstract ideas by relating them to things we can see and touch.

Metaphors play a significant role in how we understand abstract concepts. Sensory-motor metaphors, which connect abstract ideas to concrete sensory and physical experiences, consistently activate related sensory-motor areas in the brain. Although action metaphors are often studied, metaphors in other domains follow similar patterns.

Research using brain imaging, stimulation, and lesion studies suggests that when we express abstract concepts through linguistic metaphors related to sensory-motor experiences, our brains understand them in terms of those concrete experiences. These metaphors are embodied and grounded in our sensory and physical domains (Desai 2021). This understanding doesn't rely on abstract senses but rather on simulations in our action-perception systems at various levels of detail.

However, it's important to note that processing these metaphors isn't exactly the same as understanding literal concrete language. There is an abstract component involved—namely, the client's meaning-making. Abstract concepts might have independent representations that are continually shaped and enriched by these metaphors. In essence, metaphors are a powerful tool our brains use to make sense of the abstract by connecting them to our tangible experiences (Desai 2021).

You Are More Than a Walking, Talking Head

Neurocircuitry is part of the whole of you. You do not use only 20 percent of your brain—you use the whole noodle. You are interconnected to every cell in your body. Because neurons exist in your brain to the tune of 86 billion (Herculano-Houzel 2009), it's important to note that neurons also exist in other areas of your body. Your gut contains 500 million neurons (Mayer 2011), and your heart has a little brain of its own, composed of roughly forty thousand neurons (Armour 1991).

The communication among your head, heart, and gut happens through the vagal nervous system as information moves back and forth throughout your body. The vagus nerve brings somatic awareness to your brain and lets you notice sensations within your body. Like the traders on the London Stock Exchange, if you've ever had a gut feeling or your heart felt heavy or open, your somatic awareness comes from the communication among your head, heart, and gut (Porges 2011).

In this way, you can feel and sense the experience. We often rely on our minds for logic and reasoning. Our heart and gut feelings, or instincts, offer valuable insights and guidance. This continuous dialogue among the heart, gut, and brain is carried out in complex, dynamic interactions where each influences the other in both immediate and enduring ways.

Researchers from the HeartMath Institute and other organizations have found that the human heart has its own brain, or intelligence, termed the heart brain. This heart brain communicates with our primary brain, and they exchange essential information that influences bodily functions.

Although it was traditionally believed that the brain directs the body, including the heart, it's now understood that the heart also sends vital signals to the brain. The heart communicates in four primary ways: through nerve impulses, hormones and neurotransmitters, pressure waves, and electromagnetic fields. This communication profoundly affects brain activity and can also affect human performance. People can consciously influence their heart to achieve this coherent state and send positive signals throughout the body by feeling sincere, positive emotions such as compassion or appreciation (HeartMath Institute 2023).

Openhearted

Let's go back to the metaphor of the opening heart. If you breathe into the idea of an open heart, you may experience the bodily sensation of your heart opening. Strange as it may seem, your mind does not know the difference between the idea and the experience and will remember the feeling that the perceived experience creates. In broad strokes, you will experience a somatic response to the idea container of an open heart. Thus, if invited to explore the openhearted metaphor, you can embody the experience and will remember the feeling days, weeks, and even years later when you remind yourself to experience it again.

Another element related to the idea of embodiment is that your cells have memories. In the book *The Body Keeps the Score: Brain, Mind, and Body in the Healing of Trauma* (van der Kolk 2015), trauma is encoded in the memories of not only the brain but also the cells of the body. In coaching, even trauma-informed coaching, the client may not be able to safely discuss what they are experiencing.

And for many non-trauma-informed coaches, you may quickly enter unsafe territory by continually asking questions about feelings, as they can often be associated with pain and fear. Fear is not what lights up a mind to be creative in solving problems or thinking through new ways of being. Using the client's metaphors may enable them to reduce the cognitive load and create the safety and clarity of distance as they explore something. I remember a conversation with a client about moving forward after ending a difficult relationship:

Coach: What is coming to the surface for you for coaching today?

Client: Rob is being a total jerk. We're arguing about day care, pickup times, everything. I am so annoyed all the time. I really hate him. It's so overwhelming. I share a child with this idiot, and he's playing stupid games.

Coach: There is a lot there. What is most important for us to talk about, based on what you just shared?

Client: I am just so angry, and I am tired of being angry. I am in the middle of this fury tornado. I feel completely swept up by it, and at other times, I feel like I'm stuck in the eye of the storm. There's a little calm, but I know the storm will come whipping back and suck me up again, so I'm tense, my shoulders are tight, and I'm just waiting for the next thing to set it off again.

Coach: How would you like to shift your relationship to this storm?

Client: I want to be able to view it from a distance. I want to watch what is happening but still be able to be calm and let go of my anger.

Coach: Looking at it from a mile away, seeing it off in the distance?

Client: Hell no. I want to be watching it on TV from another state [laughter].

Coach: What do you notice as you watch the storm on TV from another state?

Client: I can breathe again. I can sense that the calm is more there. And I am seeing a pattern—that this isn't the first time I have dealt with this storm.

Notice the somatic embodiment of the experience of the metaphorical storm tension and the desire for calm. In asking more about how the client wants to observe the storm, she creates safety by shifting states, both literally and figuratively, so that she can look at the storm on TV. By the end of the passage, with the clarity of distance, the client can again breathe.

Going back to Chapter 1, we discussed the brain's capacity to remember imagery. The client has a visual and a visceral experience of being in the fury tornado. It is visual from the imagery of the tornado and somatic in terms of the experience of being whipped around. The metaphor allows us to stay out of the details of the situation by exploring the tornado instead of the jerky ex. If the coach asks questions that invite the client to share the blow-by-blow of how terrible Rob is, the conversation will circle the situation, and the client might try to rationalize their justified anger. Although this is interesting, it is irrelevant to the client's ability to leave the state of anger. In fact, by talking about Rob and the situation, the client is likely to whip up more fury. Conversely, by exploring how the client might want to shift her relationship to the fury tornado, she can move away from it and see it at a distance, giving her space to breathe, feel a different kind of calm, and ultimately explore those patterns that just appeared.

Another example is a client who comes to the session and talks about a lot of dissatisfaction with their life. They are doing several things, but it feels like many of them are obligations:

Client: I have this sour taste in my mouth about a lot of things in my life.

Coach: Would you say more about the sourness?

Client: It's that lemon sour. A little is good, but too much ... and it's just too much. You know what I mean?

Notice your physical response to the words *lemon sour*. Now consider what is possible if your client moves from the idea container source of sourness—"It's that lemon sour"—to a target of sour equaling not good. What if the coach hears this and leverages the recognition with curiosity?

Coach: What would you prefer to the sourness?

Client: It's not that I want the sour to all go away, but I need to add some sweetness. I want to taste sweetness in my life.

Coach: As you envision this sweet-and-sour mix, what shows up for you?

Client: I want my life to be like a big, cool lemonade [laughter].

The coach can go anywhere here, informed by this idea of a big, cool lemonade: Is it connected to the Rogerian idea of a good life? Taking the hypothesis that people often want a good life, we can be curious and begin testing the hypothesis. What are the ingredients of a big, cool lemonade? What does adding sweetness mean? What is different in how you experience your life when you taste the sweetness? What other ingredients do we need to explore? What needs to shift for the lemonade to transform into the life you want?

By exploring what your client wants in their life through the visual language of a big, cool glass of lemonade, your client begins to explore the deeper issues that might be taking away the sweetness or not bringing the sweetness. What ingredients make the lemonade sweeter? What saps the sweetness? By exploring their metaphor, their brain lights up, and so does their physical experience. They can then embody their insights about the sweetness of the lemonade. They will remember their metaphor. The lemonade is alive in their minds, and now that they are paying attention to the sweetness they want and can make choices that lead them to sweetness and ultimately meet their goal of a good life.

Not every speaker has the same meaning for the metaphor, so asking about what the client wants to do with it is crucial to understanding the context. For one person, the lemonade is what they want; for another, lemonade is what you get when all you have is lemons and you're settling. These are two very different interpretations of lemonade. The second person may want to close down their lemonade stand and get out of the business altogether. We need to avoid assumed direction regarding the metaphor; we need to ask the client, and because clients are lovely, when we ask, they will tell us. The trust and safety that you create in your willingness to be curious and to allow yourself to be led and taught by your clients results in aha moments for your clients about themselves and their experiences.

Questions

- As you reflect on this chapter, what shows up as you consider how we embody awareness and how you might use this in your coaching practice?

- The chapter discusses metaphors and their role in embodiment. How does the idea of metaphoric embodiment apply to your experiences, and how might this awareness shape how you hold the space for your clients?

- Drawing on the client-coach dialogues presented in the chapter, how might embodied cognition and somatic experiences be leveraged to facilitate a deeper understanding and meaningful change in coaching or therapeutic scenarios?

- What metaphors have your clients shared and how might you play with them to support client insights?

● What are your takeaways from this chapter?

Reading Recommendations

The Body Keeps the Score: Brain, Mind, and Body in the Healing of Trauma by Bessel van der Kolk

The HeartMath Solution: The Institute of HeartMath's Revolutionary Program for Engaging the Power of the Heart's Intelligence by Doc Childre and Howard Martin

CHAPTER 9: SOMATIC AWARENESS

" An open heart is an open mind.

—Dalai Lama XIV

Somatic awareness and the art of listening for metaphors are two of the most powerful tools in a coach's toolbox. By tapping into our physical sensations and emotions, we can unlock a deeper level of understanding and connection with our clients. This in turn enables our clients to delve into their own inner wisdom and explore their inner knowing. When people explain their somatic awareness, it often leads directly to metaphors because it is the way we tend to explain complex ideas.

As coaches, our ultimate goal is to hold the space for our clients to realize important insights. In this chapter, we will delve into how somatic awareness might appear, discovering how it can be woven into our coaching conversations and that by deepening the conversation through somatic inquiry, we ultimately open up conceptual metaphors to boot.

Presence and Somatic Awareness

Somatic awareness refers to being present in and attentive to our physical sensations and emotions. It is a form of mindfulness that lets us tune in to what is happening in our bodies and to understand how our physical experiences are connected to our thoughts and emotions. When we are somatically aware, we can identify and process our own emotions in real time, which can help us regulate our reactions and respond more effectively to challenging situations.

When you think about the idea of presence in coaching, Doug Silsbee's (2008) work on presence-based coaching is useful. Presence-based coaching is grounded in the coach's ability to be fully present and aware in the moment. This involves developing mindfulness and self-awareness and connecting with and attuning to the client's experience. Somatic awareness is key to presence and the coach's ease in evoking curiosity, creativity, and possibility. In a conversation with Bebe Hansen, MSSW, PCC, from Presence-Based Coaching, she reminded me that presence, or being present, is an inside-out experience; it's an inner state of conscious awareness, and it can be developed by our willingness to explore our habits and ways of being (Bebe Hansen, pers. comm., August 28, 2023).

What opens up in our coaching is that we are using our inside-out somatic awareness to inform our curiosity and hold space in coaching conversations. This can be powerful for connecting with your clients by helping them consider other ways of knowing. For the coach, it opens the wellspring of powerful questions that invite client awareness. This coaching emphasizes the importance of working with the whole person rather than just addressing surface-level issues. This involves exploring the client's beliefs, values, and identity, as well as their goals and challenges, and finding a way to support them in investigating these ideas with a safe lens.

Being fully present as a coach takes an embodied approach, recognizing that the mind and body are interconnected. There is a bit of a parallel process where the coach helps the client become more aware of their body and physical sensations, which can help them access their intuition and inner wisdom, while the coach uses their awareness of their body and sensations to access their intuition and inner wisdom. As either the coach or the client attunes to the body awareness, what is shared is often complex, and at that moment, most people will default to metaphors to describe it.

From this context, presence and somatic awareness are foundational for intuition. In the following coaching example, notice how the client and I explore moving from procrastination to productivity, and the somatic awareness is uncovered:

Coach: What's showing up for you that is important for a conversation today?

Client: I've recently noticed a trend where I am procrastinating more. It's almost like a lack of motivation, which is not typical for me. I'm not normally one to put things off till the last minute. So I want to get some clarity about what's happening around that.

Coach: What does it mean to procrastinate for you?

Client: When I have specific things that need to be done and I know they need to be done, and I'm like, "Meh, I'll get to that later." I mean literally doing anything other than that one thing I need to get done.

Coach: Yes. It's sort of an avoidance of doing the thing that needs to be done. If we were to get clarity on what's driving this procrastination, what would maybe make this a useful conversation today?

Client: I think, honestly, I can put things on my calendar and say I'm going to do it on this day, which I have done. And then I still procrastinate. So I think the clarity around it for me would be figuring out why I'm procrastinating. And what it is specifically around what's going on, what's different maybe? What's causing this for me right now? I think just the clarity around that would help me once I can figure out what it is, and I can do something about it. I'm not even really 100 percent sure why I'm doing it.

Coach: I'm hearing that you'd like to get some clarity around the why behind the procrastination—what is the experience you're having when you are not procrastinating.

Are things getting done the way that you would like them to be when you're doing what you need to be doing?

Client: Well, normally I'm productive. I'm trying to find the right words, I guess. I'm normally very task-oriented while still seeing the big picture because that's part of my job—to see the big picture and everything—but I'm also able to really focus. I'm very much a go-getter and on top of it. I'm able to do a lot more tasks because of the fact that I'm able to just get it done. So I guess the word would be productive.

There are places in this conversation where I could have explored the client's metaphors—for example, "I'm a go-getter," or "seeing the big picture." In that conversational moment, the client's words around procrastination and clarity seemed more powerful to me as we explored the agreement. This involved exploring the client's beliefs, values, and identity, pointed to by her words. She had made meaning around these words. Although they don't paint a visual picture like "I am a go-getter," they do carry that depth of meaning. In this conversation, I chose to explore the words. I believe it was through that exploration that we continued to delve deeply, which ultimately led to a powerful metaphor appearing later in the same conversation.

A choice point that would have supported agreement-setting and used the metaphor and thus invited deeper exploration might have been this: "Are we exploring the big picture so that you have clarity that supports you to move toward being productive?" This type of question will invite the client to explore more deeply and be more useful than addressing the surface level of how she might manage her calendar. As you will see, I didn't choose that. This also relates to the coach trusting themselves as they listen; it's not metaphors above all else. We need to be fully present and listen to what seems most important, then test the hypothesis that we are making.

Coach: So this procrastination to productivity is where the clarity needs to happen? As you think of yourself as

productive, what is standing in the way of your productivity? Just sit with that for a second. What's showing up as a place for us to explore?

Client: I find it very interesting that when you said, "What is standing in the way?," I literally got a tightening in my chest going. What is standing in the way? That's interesting to me, and I'm just like, "Ah."

Coach: Interesting.

Client: There's some stress there that I hadn't recognized until you just asked that question. When you said, "What are you noticing?," I noticed that.

Coach: Yeah, there is kind of the tightening up of your heart. Does your heart have something to share with you about that stress?

Client: I'm not sure. That's a really good question. That's not something I've thought about. I think right now, when you asked that question, the first thing that came to my mind was to be gentle—to be gentle with myself. I'm not sure why that's the first thing I thought of when you asked me what my heart needed to tell me.

Coach: Be gentle with yourself. How do you treat yourself when you feel like you're being a procrastinating person?

Client: How do I treat myself? I think that I'm significantly harder on myself than I would be to anyone else. I give a lot; I give everyone else a lot more grace than I would give myself. Because I have a lot of demands and other people's productivity depends on me. If I don't get my piece done, then they can't get their piece done. And it feels like I'm using a lot of P words today, but it feels like pressure—productivity, procrastination, and pressure, I have alliteration going there. But it feels like there's a lot of pressure, and when I don't get my pieces done, I feel like I'm letting other people down as well as myself.

Coach: As you're hearing yourself talking about the pressure and the procrastination, I'm also hearing this element of personal responsibility, and the word that's showing up is integrity. I'm curious how it lands on you.

Client: Yes. Yeah. Oh . . .

Coach: What allows you—were you about to say something? Go ahead.

Client: I was just taking a breath, literally. I wasn't about to say anything at all.

Coach: What allows for that sense of integrity?

The video of this session is on my YouTube channel under the Coaching Demonstrations section. A viewer asked about the coaching demo: "What was the clue for you through the conversation to pull up the word integrity?"

Why had integrity shown up for me? It was a good question.

My first off-the-cuff thought was, "It just bubbled to the surface for me intuitively." But the more I thought about it, I knew: It could only bubble up intuitively if something had prompted me to hear it. So I went back to the transcript. What I had keyed in on subconsciously had come from the series of responses to my questions. Words like procrastination, not typically procrastinating, lots of demands, others being dependent on her, and letting people down. Again, being present with the client allowed me to hear these words and not skip over them or try to solve them. As she had been talking, I had felt my own experience of integrity showing up in my body.

When I asked if she might answer outside of her head, the

client brought her body into the conversation when she mentioned a tightening in her heart/chest. As she continued to share how she treats herself when she considers herself to be procrastinating, I could feel my internal tension rising. I have experienced similar things and noticed that what showed up for me as she spoke was my experience of integrity. I wasn't sure, but it was an opportunity to test my hypothesis. That hypothesis became the question about the word integrity.

Client: Well, for me, it's one thing to say, "I'm going to do that," and not just do it but do it well and do it to the best of my ability. This is so bad that when I was in the Marine Corps, we always had those people who would half-ass their way through their life. And I would see people like that. I'd be like, "Yeah, they get things done. But it's just good enough. It's never above and beyond." Or it's never to the best of their ability. I mean, if that was the best of their ability, it'd be one thing. I can't imagine going through life just getting by. Just doing the bare minimum. So for me, integrity means showing up and giving my whole self. Giving all of myself to whatever it is that I'm doing. Which, right now, is impossible. I can't give myself 100 percent to everything that I'm doing because there's too much.

Coach: What does that tell you?

Client: Something has to give. I mean, and don't get me wrong, I understand when I just said that, where the pressure is coming from. You know, I'm finishing literally the last month of my MSW program. We have a lot of changes going on at work. I'm running a veterans program through the therapeutic riding program. I'm on two boards. It's too much. It's literally too much.

Coach: Yeah, that sense of overwhelm makes me curious about the expectations you have of yourself and your integrity.

Client: Right. I think that's the biggest thing right now. I'm procrastinating doing anything because I feel like I'm not doing anything well—I'm not doing any one thing well. So just don't do anything if you can't do it well [laughter].

Coach: I love the little laugh that came up. What's that?

Client: Because it's just so simple when you asked that question, and it just solidified for me. That's the problem, as I feel like I'm not doing well at anything, so just don't do anything.

Coach: Hmm.

Client: That's [cross-talk] procrastination?

Coach: Yeah. So how does that feel? I guess you may have just answered this when I was talking over you. How does that answer your why about the procrastination?

Client: Yeah, I mean, that is the why. That clarity . . . just wow. I feel I have this overwhelming sense that I'm not doing anything well. I'm kind of doing everything to just get it done instead of getting it done well. And oh, how I hate that. I hate that for myself. I want to do things to the best of my ability.

Coach: So then in reality what's stopping you from that? Let me rephrase that question: What would allow you more ease as you move toward doing the things that you're doing well and being productive?

Client: What would allow for more ease? Well, I think for me personally, I'm really focused on, of course, my last month of graduate school, and it was really—it sounds so bad—but if I could just step back from some responsibilities on the different boards. We just finished one veterans program. I'd like to wait until I've graduated before we consider starting another.

The problem is, you know, June, July, and August are prime time here in Alaska to have equine programs. So saying I need a month off would be hard.

Coach: May I share an observation?

Client: Yes.

Coach: It sounds a little binary. Are you the only person who can hold that space for three or four months?

Client: That's a good question. I don't know if we could get someone else to fill that spot. But that's a good question. And I'm taking notes now. That is actually a really good question. I think I just need that time to re-center. I hadn't considered that until you just asked that question—if it's binary. Am I the only one who can do it? I don't think so. There are lots of people who can do what I do and do it well. So finding someone to fill in for the veterans program would be a huge load off my plate right now. I can step back from the other board. Because everybody's gone fishing and camping, we don't really meet in the summer anyway, so that's about to take care of itself for a little bit. I think finding someone to fill in at least for that one space, then taking that one thing off my plate would really free up a lot of time for me to finish what I need to finish.

And, right there, a powerful conceptual metaphor showed up: "taking that one thing off my plate." This is a beautiful example of thinking is eating, which we discussed in chapter 2 on conceptual metaphors. We need to listen for those possible important sources/ targets.

In this conversation, the metaphor allowed the client to explore her full plate and also be gentle with herself. The metaphor provided the clarity of distance needed to look at the situation in a novel way, which allowed even deeper awareness. As soon as I heard this, I thought the metaphor was important, so I tested my hypothesis.

Source: Concrete Concept	Target: Abstract Concept
Overflowing Plate	Overwhelmed

Coach: Yeah. And so, as you're looking at this plate in front of you, how does it begin to look to you as you take this one element off of it?

Client: That's actually a really good visual because before it was like a Thanksgiving plate that was overflowing, and the gravy is falling off the sides.

Coach: [drip, drip, drip]

Client: And now it's like everything's just falling off the plate because you don't have room on your plate for everything. So now it's more like with just that one piece gone, everything kind of fits on the plate again. Everything has its place on the plate.

Coach: So as you look at that plate, are there any other things that maybe need to be explored for the value they offer the plate?

Client: Oh, we're looking at the protein versus the carbs, huh? Well, I think some of the things on my plate have different degrees of value to me. Of course, my graduation. And it's a month away, so that has very high value. Work—I love my work. I love my job, and it pays my bills, so that has really high value. Some of the other things on my plate don't have as high a value in that aspect. But they do have value in that they are my hobbies and my passions and something that fills my cup. So they have a different kind of value on the plate. It's like they're my veggies versus my protein. I love these food analogies we've got going on. I'm not sure how it happened. It worked for me, so I think if I was going to take anything off my plate, as far as the value-adds to the plate, I think the veterans program was the big thing. I mean, although it's incredibly important, there are other people who can fill in. I'm sure we have people who can fill in. And then for work, I actually have a really, really good team. I'm positive they'd be willing to step up and take over some of my duties just for a month so that I can get all this other stuff done. And then, honestly, that's one thing off my plate.

Coach: What just shifted in you as you're envisioning this new plate?

The metaphor is leveraged to support the client's exploration of her beliefs, values, and identity as well as her goals and challenges. As the coaching conversation continues, clarity comes from the exploration. Who hasn't ever eaten the whole plate? What did that feel like? What shifts for you if you look at that full plate and decide what you really want to eat versus trying to clean the plate? This metaphor invites the client to bring forward the somatic embodied shift in her experience: the move toward ease. It also invites the coach to stay fully present in the moment with the client.

The coach also stays with the client's stated outcome and clarity—envisioning a new plate. We don't want to lose track of what the client wants in the conversation. By linking their language to the outcome they want, the client will do the harder work in the coaching conversation.

Client: I felt at ease. I literally felt an ease, like, "It's okay. You do have a lot going on."

Coach: I saw that in the place where you had your heart tightening up. I'm seeing you go [fist clenched at heart and then opening].

Client: Yeah. I mean, because the reality is there's not enough of me to go around. I can't keep going, you know—go, go, go, go, go, go, go, go, go. Because when I say that I have a lot of responsibilities on the board for our therapeutic riding program, it's a lot. I mean, it's not just showing up to meetings; it's organizing the fundraisers, printing out the raffle tickets, verifying our insurance is paid. I mean, it's a lot; it's almost like a full-time job. And I think stepping back from that and asking others to step up in those arenas would be very helpful. We do have a vice president who can step in. And then finding someone else to run the veterans program for the summer would be phenomenal. I have a great team at work. Asking them to take on some of these duties so that I can focus on graduating—that's huge. I can actually see my plate. Not just the food.

Coach: Laughter] I love it. I love being able to see the plate. As we have this conversation, I want to see what is showing up for you as things you really want to hold on to.

Client: I think the biggest thing is asking for help. That's hard for me, and I don't know why I didn't think of that sooner. Because I know that about myself. Asking for help just to get through this hump. Because this is really just a hump. And so asking for help to get over this hump is the big thing I want to hold on to right now.

Coach: What does that tell you?

Client: It's okay to ask for help, and it's okay to need that help, and it's okay to reach out to help you over the hump.

Coach: What did you just learn about yourself as you're saying this?

Client: Boy, it sure is hard for me to ask for help. And as a professional help giver, Brené Brown would be going, "Tracey, Tracey, Tracey."

Coach: She would be like, "Girrlllfriend."

Client: She would. Oh gosh, it's like that moment of clarity when it's just something so simple that you're like, "Why couldn't you see this for yourself?"

Coach: It's hard to see a plate that's very, very full.

Client: It is. I mean, I literally have things dripping off the plate, so I need to get some things off it. Thank you.

At this point in the coaching, I shifted toward ICF core competency eight, Facilitates Client Growth. I began supporting the client to anchor awareness as she continued to use the same powerful metaphor.

Coach: Are there any actions that might support this awareness that you're now having?

Client: The first thing I'm going to do is email the team for the veterans program, and then I'm going to reach out to my boss at work to see if she can take two pieces off my plate. I thought of them as we were talking, and that will really free up enough room on my plate that I can actually see the plate. Just those things right there will help me see my plate.

Coach: Anything that might stop you or get in the way of you taking care of yourself in this way?

Client: I don't know whether it's through my own doing, but I think people have looked at me as the problem solver—"Oh, Tracey will do it." So I think setting that boundary that Tracey can't do it right now is important. I really, absolutely cannot. I think setting the boundary will be hard for me.

Coach: What might support you in being able to follow through and set the boundary for yourself?

Client: I think the visual of the plate. Understanding that right now, I'm not doing anything well. If I want to do it well, I have to have the boundary, and I have to be able to say that I can't and that my plate is full.

Coach: I think that's wonderful.

Client: Thank you.

Coach: I have this sense of a Thanksgiving meal, with that very overfull plate; I've eaten a few of those in my life. I'm having that experience of the discomfort that comes with having eaten everything on the plate versus being a bit more mindful about what I'm choosing to have on the plate. I don't know if that resonates at all or what resonates about that for you.

Client: Absolutely. I think that's overall where I am right now. It's being more mindful about what's on my plate, what's filling my cup versus overflowing my cup. And right now, my cup is overflowing. My cup overfloweth.

Coach: Are there any character strengths or values that you have and that you can use to hold yourself accountable to your agreement with yourself about taking a few things off your plate?

Client: Integrity is a really big thing for me. Being honest with myself about what I can and can't do right now is really important. Especially because everything that I'm doing is really important. There's stuff I want to do well. So that really helps me hold myself accountable to it because these things are all important and they need—they deserve—to be done well.

Coach: How did we do on getting into clarity?

Client: That it is, yeah.

Coach: Procrastination to productivity. I think that was our arc. Yes?

Client: It is our arc, and right in the middle of that is that plate! Oh my gosh, there's so much on my plate. I don't even know where to start. You know when you're at the buffet with all the desserts, and you're like, "I want one of everything," right? Instead of "Which one can I actually eat? Which one can I enjoy?"

Coach: That's a beautiful word too. How do I enjoy my plate?

Client: Yeah, because right now, I'm not enjoying my plate. I mean, literally, when we started this conversation, I was like, "Ugh," and just understanding where it's coming from and how I can fix this in the moment, I feel it. I mean, I physically feel the lightening, and it's so beautiful. Thank you for that.

Coach: You're very welcome. Is there anything you want to acknowledge yourself for as we come to a close?

Client: I just can't do it alone. I'm not an island unto myself, and I need to ask for help.

Coach: That's right. It takes a village.

Client: It does. It really does. Yes.

Coach: Does this feel like an okay place to come to a close on the conversation then?

Without the connection between the somatic awareness and the metaphor of the overflowing plate, the client might not have had such a powerful experience of what was happening to her. Exploring how to organize her calendar wouldn't have given her anything she couldn't have gotten in an organization app. Exploring integrity alone wouldn't have given the client the felt experience of understanding her why and the discomfort associated with continuing to either add things to her plate or ignoring it when it was too full. The somatic experience was explored more playfully and fully through the metaphorical language.

The Heart Brain

Beyond its pivotal circulatory functions, our heart contains about forty thousand neurons, allowing it to operate somewhat independently from our cephalic brain. Consider it an emotional processing center, deeply linked to our feelings and personal values. Communication between our heart and our head is facilitated through both electrical pathways and chemical messengers.

As we discussed in the last chapter, the discovery of the heart's little brain, or intrinsic cardiac nervous system, by Dr. Andrew Armour in 1991 was a significant breakthrough in our understanding of cardiac function and its interaction with the central nervous system. Armour's discovery of the heart's intrinsic cardiac nervous system dramatically shifted our understanding of the heart from just a pumping organ to a more complex entity with its own form of intelligence. This perspective has opened up new research dimensions in cardiology and neuroscience, emphasizing the interconnectedness of the body's systems.

There has been continued research into the gut brain as well. Our gut, surprisingly, is more than just a digestive organ—it houses approximately 100 million neurons, making it an intricate processing center. Located within the digestive tract walls, this second brain plays roles in hormone regulation, metabolism, and blood pressure stabilization. Earlier scientific beliefs posited that our central brain was the primary communicator to our gut. However, current research indicates a bidirectional communication system. Interestingly, nearly 95 percent of our serotonin, often referred to as the feel-good hormone, is found in the gut, highlighting the profound connection between gut health and emotional well-being.

Research continues with the HeartMath Institute, founded by Doc Childre in 1991. The institute is dedicated to researching and developing techniques and technologies that promote emotional well-being, stress management, and improved overall health by focusing on the connection between the heart and the brain.

In essence, HeartMath suggests that the heart is not only a

pump but also that it has its own intelligence. This heart intelligence can influence our emotional and mental states. The heart communicates with the brain and the rest of the body through a complex system of nerves and hormones (HeartMath Institute 2023).

Connecting the Dots between Somatic Experience and Metaphors

Quinn Eastman's 2012 article, "Metaphors Activate Sensory Areas of Brain," posits that the brain might use sensory memory to grasp metaphors. The study discovered that the parietal operculum—an area crucial for feeling textures—activates when we hear textural metaphors, not literal language. When a friend tells you, "I've had a rough day," notice what shows up for you. Can you feel the roughness? The brain may be replaying sensory experiences to help understand common metaphors.

The research revealed slower brain processing for metaphorical versus literal sentences. This confirmed that metaphor comprehension engages broader neural networks rather than isolated brain regions, highlighting the importance of touch in texture perception (Eastman 2012). Which also supports the somatic power of the metaphors our clients are using. In this case, thinking is feeling/experiencing.

I don't know which came first, the chicken or the egg, but I think there is something in the parable for us to consider. Multiple layers of somatic and metaphor awareness are happening in most coaching conversations. It's a delicate dance; one can never predict the order in which these elements will present themselves. Will somatic awareness take the lead, or will it be the metaphorical layer that shines through first? The beauty of coaching lies in the coach's ability to navigate these waters with fluidity, following the current of what is arising in the conversation and exploring the nuances of what the client is offering. Noticing the metaphor may lead to a deeper emotional experience or vice versa; the emotions will lead the client to make sense with imagery.

As a coach, your conversation with your client can be a labyrinth of intricate somatic and metaphorical awareness layers. By the end of this conversation, the client found that using a plate metaphor shifted her awareness and made her situation "very visual and very real." The plate became an embodied experience as she visually and physically felt the impact of eating everything on that full plate. This conversation occurred spontaneously by actively listening to what was showing up in the space. It was generated by listening and then playing with and exploring the client's visual language, being curious, and investigating the client's words and meaning in new and novel ways, giving her space to explore new conceptualizations of her situation.

Questions

- How does the integration of somatic awareness in coaching conversations contribute to a more holistic approach to client understanding?

- What is the connection between somatic awareness, presence-based coaching, and the capacity to evoke curiosity, creativity, and possibility in a coaching session?

- How might a coach use their own somatic awareness to connect more deeply with their clients and facilitate exploration of their beliefs, values, and identity?

- Why do you think people often use metaphors to describe their somatic awareness?

Reading Recommendation

Presence-Based Coaching: Cultivating Self-Generative Leaders through Mind, Body, and Heart by Doug Silsbee

Chapter 10: The Coaching Competencies

" You have two ears and one mouth; use them accordingly.

—Stephen Covey

If you are a coach with the ICF, you will be familiar with the ICF core competencies. They were updated at the end of 2019/early 2020. The ICF reduced the prior eleven competencies to eight core competencies that are essential for professional coaches. They are designed to provide a framework for the coaching container. They ultimately support coaches to hold a conversational container for effective practices. In this chapter, we will briefly outline the eight competencies to ensure that we are on the same page.

Competency 1: Code of Ethics

Definition: Understands and consistently applies coaching ethics and standards of coaching.

There are many elements that, although important, are more about how we function as coaches, communicating transparently with our clients and potential clients—how we navigate confidentiality, financial agreements, roles and responsibilities, and conflicts of interest that may arise in a coaching engagement.

In the ICF code of ethics, some elements point to how we

engage with the person in front of us. One area is the cultural competency of embracing diversity and valuing the richness of our clients' experiences. As a coach, we will continue our development with self-awareness, self-monitoring, and self-improvement.

Several key definitions include the following (ICF 2020):

- "Coaching—partnering with clients in a thought-provoking and creative process that inspires them to maximize their personal and professional potential."

- "Equality—a situation in which all people experience inclusion, access to resources and opportunity, regardless of their race, ethnicity, national origin, color, gender, sexual orientation, gender identity, age, religion, immigration status, mental or physical disability, and other areas of human difference."

Both of these definitions point to a foundational principle in coaching—specifically, they are both relevant to coaching with metaphors. When you drop the need to be the expert, you open yourself to learning from your client. Through this partnership, you cannot help but treat people with cultural competence. Chapter 14 will explore this in more depth.

Competency 2: Embodying a Coaching Mindset

Definition: Develops and maintains a mindset that is open, curious, flexible, and client-centered.

Again, this isn't a deep dive into every element of this newest core competency, the coaching mindset. Instead, it is a quick look at how metaphors effortlessly bring forward aspects of this competency. The coach has a "mindset that is open, curious, flexible, and client-centered" (ICF 2020b). Metaphors show a place where the open, curious, flexible, client-centered coach can shine.

A coaching mindset is a process that requires ongoing learning and development along with the coach establishing a reflective practice for their work. Self-reflection is pivotal to how we learn to listen differently. I still run coaching conversations through RaeNotes to highlight my questions, metaphors that I maybe didn't hear, possible important underlying issues and themes, possible desired outcomes, and success measures my clients may have shared. Reflection is key to consciously and intentionally improving your coaching.

Competency 3: Establishes and Maintains Agreements

Definition: Partners with the client and relevant stakeholders to create clear agreements about the coaching relationship, process, plans, and goals. Establishes agreements for the overall coaching engagement as well as those for each coaching session.

There are two areas to cover here. There is the overarching goal(s) of the work that you are doing with a client. This overarching goal (macro) is what you may be exploring throughout the coaching engagement. We discuss this more in chapter 12 with the embodied grounded goals.

There are also agreements in every individual coaching conversation you have within the larger engagement. Agreements are crucial to creating a container for the coaching conversation. Without a strong agreement, it is very difficult for a coach to demonstrate any of the other competencies well. What often happens without a strong agreement is a delightful, winding conversation, often with a coach trying to "understand" the context and solve problems for another person. It might be somewhat useful but often is two people out in a field wandering around trying to discover something important.

With a strong agreement, the coach asks questions to invite the client to name what is important to be explored in the conversation. These types of questions prime both the client and the coach to what is important and where they are going to start exploring.

- What is bubbling up as most important for us to discuss today?
- You shared several directions we might explore. Which one is more meaningful today?
- What would be different for you at the end of our session if we

fully explored X?

- How would you know we had gotten where you want to be by the end of our session?
- What is showing up as important between where you are now and where you want to be at the end of the session?

These are not absolutes, yet they do point to the coach inviting the client to name what is important, what they want by the end, and where and how they want to explore what they say is important to them.

Competency 4: Cultivates Trust and Safety

Definition: Partners with the client to create a safe, supportive environment that allows the client to share freely. Maintains a relationship of mutual respect and trust.

In some ways, this competency is the most misunderstood. For many people, the idea of trust and safety has to do with the warmth or openness of the coach—that the client feels safe. There are many coaches who are very nice, and niceness does engender some feelings of safety. But trust and safety are determined more by the coach's actions and words being in alignment with the client's.

If I say, "Coaching is a partnership where I support you to find your own answers" and then act by telling you where to look and how to focus, start giving you homework, and basically dump all my expertise on you, it doesn't generate trust. Sit with that for a moment. If I tell you what to do instead of asking you what is important to you, how well do you trust me?

When your client shares a powerful feeling, belief, story, or the like, notice it. They are demonstrating trust by sharing; you are demonstrating trust by acknowledging and being curious to learn more about them and how they make meaning.

Consider how you feel if, instead of telling you anything, I ask you open-ended questions that only you can answer. If I ask you for direction on what is important to you, how you would like to explore what is important to you, and use your words, visual language, and worldview to show I am curious about you and on your behalf, what do you notice now about feeling trust?

Psychological safety is crucial in any environment where learning and growth are valued. It refers to the feeling of being able to express oneself without fear of judgment, ridicule, or punishment. When people feel safe to take risks and be vulnerable, they are more likely to be open, curious, and receptive to new ideas. This is the foundation of the competency of trust and safety, not just being a warm, nice person.

Competency 5: Maintains Presence

Definition: Is fully conscious and present with the client, employing a style that is open, flexible, grounded, and confident.

Going back to what we discussed in chapter 9 on presence, this is about who you are being with your clients. The coach responds to what the client brings forward, letting go of assumptions about what they need to do or how the client needs to be doing it.

By our capacity to hold the space, we encourage self-discovery: Rather than offering advice or solutions, presence in coaching focuses on giving the client ample room to discover their own insights and solutions. The coach serves as a partner in curiosity, helping the client to explore their experience and gain new perspectives.

The coach honors what the client names as important. A hallmark is when you can demonstrate radical unattached curiosity or, as I think about it, compassionate detachment. (I'll write more about compassionate detachment in chapter 16.) The idea is that we aren't attached to the finding or to fixing the client or the outcomes. Solutions and outcomes are the work of the client, not the coach. Although the coach is free to share observations, doing so with open hands and zero attachment to being right is key to how we hold the space for others to grow.

One of the difficult qualities of coaching presence is the capacity to sit in silence—asking a question and then letting the client take the time to ponder, process, and answer it. The coach lets go of the need to fill silence with sound. Allow space that gives clients room to think, create and connect dots, make new dots, and then develop their insights.

Competency 6: Listens Actively

Definition: Focuses on what the client is and is not saying to fully understand what is being communicated in the context of the client systems and to support client self-expression.

Listening actively is about the coach's ability to understand the client's communication and fully support their self-expression. This involves customizing questions and observations based on what you have learned about the client and their situation, exploring the words and emotions the client shares, and being attentive to the client's energy shifts, nonverbal cues, and behaviors. The coach should also let the client speak without interruption and succinctly reflect or summarize what the client communicated to ensure their clarity and understanding.

Many times when I ask a question, the client sighs heavily, makes a face, starts laughing, or rubs their head. All of these are beautiful opportunities to invite curiosity. What just happened there? In this way, we are listening far below the surface to the unconscious that appears in front of us.

Competency 7: Evokes Awareness

Definition: Facilitates client insight and learning by using tools and techniques such as powerful questioning, silence, metaphor, or analogy.

This is a favorite competency for many coaches, including myself, because listening for metaphors is my favorite tool. Yet evoking awareness involves the coach as the tool. I love saying, "You are the tool." The most useful training is not about using worksheets but how it supports coaches to use their expertise to inform their curiosity. Through the use of inquiry, the coach can facilitate the client's insight and learning.

The coach as the tool includes powerful questioning, silence, and the use of metaphors or analogies. The coach asks questions that help the client explore their current way of thinking and feeling and their values, needs, wants, beliefs, or behaviors. Coaches also ask questions to support clients in considering new or expanded ways about themselves or their situation. The coach may share observations or thoughts without attachment and invite the client's exploration. Lastly, the coach learns to ask clear, direct, primarily open-ended questions at a pace that allows for reflection while using concise language, which lets the client to do most of the talking.

Coaching focuses on facilitating deeper understanding and insight for the client. The aim is to help the client explore their current mindset and emotional state, their self-concept (the who), their specific circumstances (the what), and the outcomes they wish to achieve.

In supporting the client in achieving their desired outcomes, the coach employs a multilayered approach to questioning that prompts the client to consider new modes of thinking, feeling, or behaving. This can be done playfully with metaphors. As the client describes their full plate or feeling like they're running on a hamster wheel, the coach can use metaphors to invite the client into deeper awareness. By using these metaphors as jumping-off points, the coach invites the client to delve into a deeper level of awareness. Questions like, "As you look at this plate, what do you notice is important?" or "What would you like to do with the hamster wheel?," serve to evoke a form of awareness that only the client can provide, enriching the coaching partnership and empowering the client in their journey of self-discovery.

Competency 8: Facilitates Client Growth

Definition: Partners with the client to transform learning and insight into action. Promotes client autonomy in the coaching process.

This involves the coach partnering with the client to transform their learning and insight into action while promoting their autonomy in the coaching process. In competency eight, facilitating client growth serves as the anchoring of transformative change. This competency ensures that the seeds of self-awareness sown in the present session and in earlier sessions blossom into concrete actions and habits. Adept coaches understand that their role is to act as a partner in this process, fostering an environment where the client is the primary agent of their own growth. They are fully capable of coming up with actions that support their insights.

Competency eight is also the closing of the coaching container; we have primed the conversation in agreement-setting:

- "What would be different at the end of this conversation?"
  - ▼ "I would have tools."
- "How would tools impact you?"
  - ▼ "I would be more confident."
- "Is that what we are doing today, moving toward confidence in using your tools?"
  - ▼ "Yes."

Now, at the end of the container, these are the questions to ask:

- "How did we do in exploring confidence?"
  - ▼ "We did XYZ."
- "What tools are showing up that might be useful to play with?
  - ▼ "XYZ."
- What have you learned about yourself or been reminded of in our conversation?"
  - ▼ "XYZ."
- "What actions will support that insight or awareness?"
  - ▼ "XYZ."

The coach is empowering the client to name for themselves their insights, the actions that align with their insights, and the tools they will use to achieve what they want.

By encouraging the client to consider how they will use their new learning from the session and partnering with them to design post-session thinking, reflection, or action, the coach supports agency. In addition, the coach partners with the client to consider how to move forward, including identifying resources, support, or potential barriers. Clients are invited to design the best methods of accountability for themselves. Coaches celebrate their progress and learning and partner with the client on how they want to complete the session.

The Container of a Coaching Conversation

With this outline of the competencies, we have a framework for coaching—the container of a coaching conversation. These competencies are not meant to be a rigid formula but rather the fundamentals that support a coach to hold the space in such a way that their clients have insights that empower them to make meaning and choices that are encouraged by their own voice.

Metaphors weave seamlessly through every competency as we leverage the clients' metaphors to create a container and explore the deeper important issues below the surface. When we learn how to use the metaphors that appear, we can demonstrate more than one competency. Agreement-setting, trust and safety, presence, listening, evoking awareness and, ultimately, facilitating client growth all benefit from using the clients' metaphors and language. Metaphors truly can find their way into every competency. As the coach, it's your job to tune your ears to hear them and then use them to support your clients' insights, empowerment, and the actions that will move them toward what they want.

Questions

- How does the competency of establishing and maintaining agreements contribute to creating a strong container for coaching conversations?

- What competency do you naturally demonstrate, and which do you need to play with more in your coaching?

- Why is cultivating trust and safety essential in coaching, and how does it go beyond simply being a warm and nice person?

- How can coaches demonstrate trust through their questions?

- What is a takeaway from this chapter?

Reading Recommendation

Coach the Person, Not the Problem: A Guide to Using Reflective Inquiry by Dr. Marcia Reynolds

Chapter 11: Metaphors & the Coaching Container

" Life is a journey. Time is a river. The door is ajar.

—Jim Butcher

I mentioned earlier my experience working with Rape Crisis and how that formed much of the focus of my work around client empowerment and agency. The understanding of how important it is to give people back their power was an experience that formed how I thought about empowerment and the role I wanted to play in working with people. That experience set me on the path toward social work and, ultimately, coaching.

I align deeply with the idea that people are whole, capable, resourceful, and creative. They have within them the answers to their own struggles. The struggle is where their learning lives. My job is not to solve their life; instead, I see myself as a short-term solution for their long-term life. I want my clients to be empowered. "Give a person a fish, and you feed them for a day. Teach a person to fish, and you feed them for life." I am more interested in supporting client agency and autonomy, not setting up a fish shop.

These concepts are fundamental to the coaching framework. Using the clients' language is key to powerful coaching. Using metaphors is the conduit to giving clients back their power, deeply listening, exploring how they perceive the world, and respecting their unique insights into the coaching process. It has also become how we have the most fun together as we tackle complex, tender, painful, and exciting issues.

Session Goals

One thing that makes the core competencies fit within the dynamics of how the brain works is the idea of priming. If we prime our brain toward some direction, we stand a much better chance of reaching what we say we want. Stephen Covey says to "begin with the end in mind." One of the purposes of agreement-setting in individual coaching sessions is to begin creating the coaching container of the conversation. We need to know what is important to the client, not just their topic but what is really meaningful for the discussion we're about to have. We need to begin with the end in mind so that both the client and the coach have an idea of what would be different at the end of their time together.

As described in the last chapter, a strong agreement in a coaching conversation makes demonstrating all the other competencies easier. If you have ever been in a coaching conversation where you and your client were lost in the weeds somewhere, you have probably bypassed a strong agreement and don't have clarity and alignment around what was important to the client and what they wanted to have by the end of the session.

One of my mentor coaches, Jan Berg, MCC, reminded me years ago that agreement-setting is, in fact, coaching. This is an important reminder because coaches often want to move quickly through the agreement-setting and get to the "real" coaching.

Let's put this in the framework of you coming to visit me at my home. You've driven to my house, and let's say I live somewhere you've never visited before, and you want to see the sights. After the pleasantries have taken place and we are sitting in your car with your hands on the wheel, we're ready to explore. What is your first question? "Where are we going?" Most likely followed very quickly by your second question: "How do we get there?"

Agreement-setting isn't rocket science; you do this all the time. You talk to people and ask for directions. If you don't, it's a good time to start. It's a critical coaching skill. This is elemental to setting the agreement. Clients will tell us, usually in the first five minutes of a conversation, what is really important to them. It is crucial that a coach is not thinking about what question they need to ask next to evoke awareness or focusing on details about the situation but is instead leaning into their capacity for coaching presence and taking the time needed to get clarity and alignment on what is important to the client and where they want to be at the end of the conversation.

Plates appear a lot in coaching, and you can see the similarities and differences in the next coaching demonstration. Let's explore it and work through all the competencies.

Agreement-Setting

Coach: What is showing up as important to explore today?

Client: Lately, I have been in a space of hurry up and wait for a lot of different things. And now a lot of things are converging all at the same time. I'm finding myself in the space where I have too much on my plate when I've been waiting for something to be on my plate. Specifically, I have found myself in a partnership and feel like I can't decide whether or not it's fruitful. I'm trying to figure out what to do because I have so many things on my plate. I feel like I've been really mindful about what I'm saying yes and no to.

As noted earlier, in most coaching conversations, the client will share the important, meaningful issue in the first five minutes. In this session, they mention the metaphor of a full plate three times as well as trying to figure out what is fruitful. Going back to the conceptual metaphors in the previous example, the conceptual metaphor has appeared as a full plate as the source and overwhelm as the target. It is pointing to what is important—the client experiencing overwhelm in choosing. The coach still needs to reconfirm (test the hypothesis) what the client wants to explore. Yet exploring the plate will be more fun for the client than specifically explaining a lot of details to the coach about the business choices.

This example also demonstrates how a coach might begin exploring what would be different at the end of the conversation—creating a metaphorical container. Let's look at agreement-setting through this lens, continuing with the previous example.

Coach: When you look at this really full plate, given that we're going to be talking for fifteen to twenty minutes, what would you like us to do with this plate by the end of our conversation?

The coach uses the metaphor to confirm what the client wants to explore and also asks for a success measure. The question is client-centered and client-led, as the coach uses the metaphor lighting up the client's brain and then asking what would change or be different. In this way, the client is making the choice, and the metaphorical language is neutral and nondirective. The client is deciding what is important for the conversation.

Client: I think it would be helpful to clarify one or two things that I could at least say no to today.

Coach: When you look at that plate, where should we start exploring? Before you answer that, I have another question: When you look at that plate, are there things on it that are low-hanging fruit that we could explore first?

In this example, we now have discovered what the client wants to explore, what is important to have at the end of the conversation, and the metaphorical conduit the client's brain brought forward. The coach is also partnering with the client to determine how they would like to explore this in the rest of the conversation. In the next chapter, I will use the remainder of this conversation to demonstrate how this agreement set up the coach and client to fully explore her topic so that she dove way below the waterline. She and the coach both showed up as mermaids, fearlessly ready to dive below the waterline into what is driving her choices.

Trust, Presence, Awareness, and Growth

Psychological safety is crucial in any environment where learning and growth are valued. In this coaching demonstration, the client stated at the end that she was worried that the coaching was going to focus on her failing, but we never went to failing because we were just looking at a plate. The metaphor created the clarity of distance that allowed for psychological safety and then the client's willingness to talk and take some risks.

We know that when people feel vulnerable or self-conscious, they may have difficulty finding the right words to describe their experiences. Metaphors let people convey their ideas and emotions through a more imaginative and creative lens, making sharing feel safer.

A brain that feels safe is more open to exploring and questioning itself from the shoreline of a psychologically safe environment. People speak up and share their thoughts and ideas, question themselves, look at their own thinking, and get curious about the connections and stories they are telling themselves. It's through this curiosity that our clients will discover the steps that will lead them toward their goals.

For example, if someone feels overwhelmed about what to say yes or no to, they might use the metaphor of having a full plate to describe their experience. It captures the intensity and urgency of their feelings, allowing them to express their struggles in a less direct and potentially less intimidating way.

As with most things, the competencies don't live in silos, separate from each other; they are threads that weave together to form a comprehensive learning experience. When used with artfulness, the competencies support client agency and invite client awareness. The coach holds the curiosity but not the answers. From this perspective, you create trust and safety by partnering, presence, listening, evoking awareness, and letting the client guide you through their internal landscape.

Listening actively, being fully present as a partner to the client, and evoking awareness are not three individual tasks; they are interdependent in a full coaching conversation. The client experiences the coach acknowledging them and asking simple, open-ended questions that don't have an obvious conclusion. This demonstrates to the client that they are taking the lead and that the coach is walking alongside them. The coach and client demonstrate being in full partnership.

Coach: When you look at this really full plate, given that we're going to be talking for fifteen to twenty minutes, what would you like us to do with this plate by the end of our conversation?

Client: I think it would be helpful to clarify one or two things that I could at least say no to today.

Coach: When you look at that plate, where should we start exploring? Before you answer that, I have another question: When you look at that plate, are there things on it that are low-hanging fruit that we could explore first?

Client: Well, I have one partnership that I like. I had an opportunity to join friends who are starting a consulting firm, and I was really excited about it at first. But the more I get into it, the more I have a lot of questions that feel unresolved.

The metaphors support the client's brain because they come from her mind. The plate and what would be fruitful make sense to the client because it's how she is already experiencing her situation. Using the metaphor and then asking how she would like to explore gives her the choice to decide what low-hanging fruit she might like to start with. The coach is maintaining presence with not knowing. There is no way we would know what the low-hanging fruit might be.

Being acknowledged and having the support to express any direction, feelings, perceptions, concerns, or beliefs is empowering. The client and the coach are in full partnership. The client has the agency to respond in any way that makes sense to her. And the question the coach brought forward comes directly from the client's words. The coach demonstrates more than trust and safety with these open, client-based questions.

When you use the clean language of metaphors, you are responding to your client as a whole person. You demonstrate curiosity and comfort with not knowing or needing to drive the client toward a specific outcome. Metaphors keep us from solving problems and pushing clients in any direction other than into their own knowledge and insights.

Client: Well, I have one partnership that I like. I had an opportunity to join friends who are starting a consulting firm, and I was really excited about it at first. But the more I get into it, the more I have, not a hard no, but a lot of questions that feel unresolved.

Coach: Do you have a sense of what's important, of what's driving that discomfort or that uncertainty?

Client: It feels like there's constant conflict that doesn't need to be there.

Coach: What would you need to be a hard yes?

Client: Like to keep it?

Coach: Yeah. I'm just curious. What would need to be different if you were to keep it?

Client: Well, that's the part that I'm not sure of. I don't know if this is reasonable, but it feels like in my life right now, I want things that are easy and/or entirely enjoyable. I'm in the season of my life where either I enjoy them fully or I want to live in my superpowers, you know?

Coach: What does it tell you when you hear yourself say that in regard to this situation?

Client: It feels like that's 100 percent not the situation [laughter]. It doesn't fit either criteria. Then I'm questioning, "Is that criteria reasonable? Is that reasonable?"

Coach: That's a really, really interesting question. How do you know if it's reasonable or not to have that requirement?

Client: I don't know because it feels like the old adage, "If you find something you love, you'll never work a day in your life." It feels like even that doesn't seem reasonable because all work is work.

Coach: That's interesting.

Client: For instance, I'm doing this coaching training. And let's say I enjoy it by the end of this training, and I love it so much that I moved my entire life to just full-time coaching. There's going to be some kind of bookkeeping I'm going have to do. I would rather not do that. But there's going to have to be a section of my life that's keeping track of paperwork, right?

Coach: May we go back to the plate real quick?

Client: Sure.

In this part of the conversation, real work is beginning to happen. From the safety of the plate, the client can begin to assess how she makes choices about what she does or doesn't want. And the awareness that she's not even thinking about her own plate in how she makes the decisions is crucial to why the decision doesn't feel aligned. From our early exploration of our senses, the client's head, heart, and gut are out of alignment with her actions. If the coach just told her, "You need to put yourself on the plate," there would be the inherent judgment that she's doing it wrong. Then her brain might shut down, and the coaching would be less useful.

Part of what makes this work is that the coach isn't attached or determining the direction; they stay in open curiosity and wonder. From their external position, they can use all they know—all the theory, all the neuroscience, and all their expansive training—not to give the answer but to inform their curiosity on behalf of the client.

The metaphor is also used to check in with the client and to continue exploring the deeper issues. How does the client determine something? If we ask about the situation, they are going to dive into explaining what is and isn't working, and there will be rationalizations as to why they should or shouldn't keep doing what they are doing. But by returning to the plate, the coach uses a different approach, and the question is about how the client makes decisions, not about people but about things on a plate.

Coach: When you look at this idea of coaching being the plate, there are going to be some things on the plate that maybe you don't love. But there are other things on the plate that you may love a lot. How do you determine when there's enough of what you love versus how much you don't love on the plate that makes it what you want to do? How do you make that determination?

Client: Looking wholly at the plate like a balanced meal?

Coach: I don't know. Is that what you do?

Client: I've never had the luxury of looking at my plate like that. It's kind of been like you're eating gruel. Be thankful you're eating, you know? And that's, I think, two pieces. Number one, is it even realistic criteria? Number two, it seems almost like a luxury to even be taking the time to be choosy about that. Like, who are you to even be choosy about that?

This is a particularly interesting insight into how someone has an unconscious story: "Who are you to be choosy? Eat what's on your plate." Look at how that story is now impacting a business decision twenty-five to thirty years later. This is an example of why it's imperative to explore the metaphor, because if what we were doing instead was making a decision tree about the pros and cons of a decision, we would never have gotten below the waterline to what is driving the impasse regarding making the decision in the first place. It's only by exploring through a new lens that the client begins to capture the deeper awareness, thoughts, and values that are being impacted by the decision to be made.

Coach: I'm really curious because when we started, there was also a sense of moving toward how do you know to let go of something that might be on this plate. I'm hearing, and I could be wrong, so please correct me if I'm wrong, but I'm also hearing that when you have an opportunity to really look at the plate you'd like to have in front of you, there's a bit of discomfort with just going, "That's the plate I want."

Client: Hmm.

Coach: What are you noticing as I say that?

Client: Well, I think it's two things. One, I think the second that I say I have told you that I would like to do something with you, and then I do it, and I'm like,

"Never mind," I think there's a lot of like, "I'm really attached to being a person of my word." And so, even if I'm like you and I know us working together is not working, bigger than that is me being a person of my word.

Coach: Oh.

Client: And then the other piece is me having a plate that I desire and love. That comes secondary to obligations that the plate funds and supports.

Coach: It's sort of interesting because we had a very interesting conversation earlier today around recontracting, and I'm curious, is there a place between where you have a new need to recontract, so what do you do? What's between this idea that my word means my bond is forever to the detriment of the plate that I prefer to have?

Client: Yeah...

Coach: That's a face?

The client is having a somatic response to the question. It's showing up as a very dramatic face. If the coach ignores this, it's a missed opportunity.

Client: That's the face I make when my brain explodes [laughter]. And then I'm like, "I don't know what that means." Yeah, it would be shifting what it means to have a plate to begin with. And that's because then it would mean the plate could actually be a plate that's enjoyable. And then it could mean that lives won't end if I just have a conversation with you and say, "Hey, I know that we showed up in this with the whole full understanding, and it's time to renegotiate that." And that it's not me failing my word. It's actually just me renegotiating.

Coach: Again, I could be wrong, but it seems there was an energy shift as you said that. What did you notice inside of yourself as you said that out loud?

Client: Freedom. Literally like my whole energy did shift and change. Even talking about it before, I felt like bondage and like failure. I felt failure. This entire conversation, I was like, "I don't want to talk about failing." And then you're like, "What if you renegotiated that?" And I was like, "Oh well, I could just renegotiate everything then."

You and your client can explore deeply using the metaphor framework. The conversation doesn't have to be formal or perfect; it should be real and in the moment. This type of discussion builds trust and safety, which is crucial for real change to take place. When your client has a physical experience of their awareness—"That's the face I make when my brain explodes"—these are not just words: It's the facial expression and the way a body experiences insight. This type of mental, emotional, and somatic awareness is hard to forget and will stay with your client even after the conversation has ended.

Facilitates Client Growth

The coach can continue to connect with the client using the metaphor and also invite the client to consider how they will do what is needed from the insights they just experienced. The client then can develop their own actions, that align with and make sense, given the insights they just had.

Coach: What does that look like when you renegotiate this plate?

Client: That almost means that everything is up for discussion then. It's almost like I have this contract, right? And the contract is that you do things out of obligation. You do things and you're tied to pleasing other people. So like every item on the contract, if we're going to renegotiate the one thing, then you might as well renegotiate the whole thing. Right? So it was like this liberation that happened

Coach: So what is the thing that you need to take off the plate? [Big swipe with my hand, like clearing off the plate.]

Client: Yeah. Cool. Um, shit [laughter]. Yeah. The everything.

Coach: The everything

Client: Like the load—the load entirely. I feel like everything. I think I have to clear the plate and renegotiate everything because the plate under new terms might look very similar. But I think everything right now is on there with a certain understanding that I no longer want to hold.

Coach: Is there a value or a character strength that you can use to support yourself in holding yourself accountable to this awareness?

Client: Yeah, loyalty. I think loyalty is one of my highest values, but I've always interpreted it as loyalty to other people instead of like a loyalty to self-care. Not self-preservation, because that's like survivalist, but like loyalty to my thriving and well-being.

Coach: What's the first thing that you might need to do with this plate?

Client: Dump it [laughter]. No, I think the first thing I need is to get a divided dish. I hate my food to touch [laughter]. Super gross. But in reality, though, a divided dish because I think that would help me be really honest about what can fit on it. Because the divided dishes have portions, right, and it's like there are six containers or whatever, and then when I go into it, I can say, "Oh, you want to work together? Cool. Well, I only have three containers left." So let me be really honest about that commitment. And where I'm at, what I'm thinking, and what I'm feeling.

Coach: How do you do that then? I mean, I'm looking at the time, so I want to see if there's something that you can really walk away from this conversation with that is an action for you to take. What would that be?

Client: I think it would be to get a divided dish. And then also because you referenced our conversation from before. Sometimes you move from contracts to month to month, right? And I think I've been managing my plate like a lifelong contract. And so maybe looking at my plate as a divided dish instead of just like a buffet plate piled with food. Ugh. So a divided dish and then also thinking about it more, like a month-to-month kind of situation. So it's more like, "Yes, and we'll see how it goes." Right? But that's never been a factor for me.

Coach: How does this feel? Do you feel like we got something off your plate?

Client: You . . . I'm not even being funny. You transformed my life.

In this short coaching demonstration, you can see how using metaphors allows for clean, concise, and neutral language that gives your client plenty of space to explore meaning. The coach demonstrates holding space for the client without judgment and stays curious in the place of not knowing.

Along the way, the coach checks in with the client and invites them to look at what else is on their plate. Metaphors can help your client capture learning and create actions, which ultimately supports them in creating their own accountability as they develop next steps that align with their insights and forward movement.

Also, by listening for and leveraging metaphors, you can elevate your capacity to demonstrate the competencies at a very high level. Even more importantly, this artful coaching can help you support your clients as they move toward empowered agency, letting them take charge of their growth and development.

Questions

- As you reflect on this chapter, what do you notice as you consider how the competencies are demonstrated in multiple ways using metaphors?

- How does the use of metaphors contribute to creating trust and safety in the coaching relationship?

- What benefit do you see in using the client's metaphor to check in with how the coaching conversation is going?

- What was your best learning in this chapter?

Recommended Reading

The ICF Core Competencies, by the International Coaching Federation

The 2020 PCC Markers, by the International Coaching Federation

Chapter 12: Embodied Grounded Goals

" Those who have a "why" to live, can bear with
almost any "how."

—Viktor E. Frankl, *Man's Search for Meaning*

When I started coaching, I worked with people to create goals that excited them and that we could break down into baby steps. The premise was that we needed a goal worthy of coaching. My clients come up with all sorts of things they want:

- "I want to improve my leadership skills."
- "I want a successful business."
- "I need a clear plan for my business."
- "I need to lose weight."
- "I want to have confidence."
- "I want to have next steps."
- "I want work-life balance."

Although all of these are fine, none of them light up a brain with excitement. One of the things I noticed was that people had hit-or-miss success with these goals. Even for the ones that sounded like fun—"I want balance in my life"—something was missing. What does it mean to have balance? How do you know when you are experiencing balance? What is the image that speaks to you of balance? If you were to embody balance, what would be different? What allows you to be in balance?

There were a lot of unasked questions and, in hindsight, the thing that was missing was the idea of an embodied grounding goal (EGG) or statement. Something that the person was excited by and could remember after the session, and it needed to lead to the embodied state they wanted to live in.

Overarching Goals

As I continued to work with people, I started to use the language of grounding goals or statements. I wanted the goal to be an outcome and something the client loved to say to themselves. Part of the success of any goal is that it is alive in us.

So I tweaked my language. The goal was necessary, but the felt experience that the client wanted was even more critical. Remember, people naturally default to metaphors when communicating complex ideas. The visual language of metaphors is easy to remember. I wanted my clients to have a statement that served not only the goal: They needed a goal that was alive for them at the moment when life went off the rails. If the EGG is powerful enough for the client, they could use the statement as a touchstone to reorient themselves. They needed to fully own and know the goal statement.

The more I worked with my clients, the more the EGG started to sound like the following:

- "I live a life of perpetual awesomeness."

- "Confidently, I move forward into the unknown."

- "I show up for my organizational peers and team like I show up for my customers."

- "I have confidence in the gray space."

- "I move in ways that honor the seven generations."

- "Grounded, I confidently communicate my truth."

- "Courageously, I hold the space for truth and transparency with my team."

I have discovered that, first, the EGGs are metaphorical in nature and, second, that the client owns them. These sorts of goals are the umbrella, an overarching desire that every other thing the client is struggling with nestles under. The themes of being a good leader, a visionary, creative, losing weight, finding balance, finding confidence, being entrepreneurial, and having a good life all fit under the EGG.

For me, "I am deep belly laughs" reorients me from all the little things that might bog me down—anger, fear, speaking up or not speaking up, writing or not writing, unrealistic expectations, criticism, taking myself too seriously, choices I made that I wish I hadn't. All of these fit as topics under the larger goal of living as if "I am deep belly laughs." This is not solely a coaching goal but a lifelong goal. "I am deep belly laughs" grounds me and is also the energy I want to share and live into. I feel the laughter bubble up from my belly and into my heart each time I say this to myself. It is easy to remember, even when the world might feel like it is spinning off its axis, such as when I look at a blank page and wonder what to write or if anyone will read it.

Given that people seek out a coach to overcome some struggle, there tend to be themes around feeling stuck and wanting confidence, empowerment, balance, and trust in themselves. If your clients can't remember their big, juicy, deeper goal or use it to reorient themselves daily, it may not be working as well as it could, and it is definitely not embodied.

The concept of the EGG emphasizes the significance of rooting goals in a combination of cognitive, emotional, and physical states. Unlike traditional goal-setting approaches that may be overly rational or detached from emotional and bodily experience, EGGs provide a holistic approach that engages your entire being—mind, body, and spirit.

These are goals that truly ignite our passion, and they are not just conceived in the mind but are birthed from the heart, nurtured by our actions, and live as vibrant metaphors in our everyday life. As a coach, how do you answer this question yourself? What is your big, juicy, embodied goal? What grounds you when you are at the mercy of the winds of life? What goals ignite your passion?

Creating an EGG

In this example, I will share how I worked with a client to capture the overarching goal for our sessions. The client and I were discussing the larger issue they wanted to address in the coaching. There was a feeling that what they wanted to do in the world was so big that it was hard to remember in difficult moments. There was a need to align with who they wanted to be and how they wanted to show up.

This impacted how the client was first making choices and then finding the motivation to take action on those choices.

As we began, I asked the client if it was okay for me to take notes in the chat so that I could share with her the words I was capturing. That is what I do in my first session with clients.

Client: I want a goal that speaks to who I want to be.

Coach: If I can, I'd like to take notes in the chat as you're talking so that I can start to capture things that you're saying as you're speaking, unless it bothers you. If you can ignore the little pop-up chat thing down below, I will ask you about the things that I'm hearing along the way. I will pause and ask you to reflect on what you've shared, to pull out the essential elements for crafting this goal. What's showing up for you as a place to start as we begin to explore this grounded and embodied goal?

Client: In my personal journey, my ultimate goal is to help raise the frequency of the planet. I acknowledge that this is a colossal aim. To manifest it, I am committed to guiding people toward making empowered choices and to help them reframe how they look at themselves and look at life. And to get to a place of inner permission, where they give themselves permission in being more of themselves.

Notes in the chat box:

» 00:10:26 Lyssa deHart: Help support raising the frequency of the planet

» 00:10:40 Lyssa deHart: Empowered choice

» 00:10:52 Lyssa deHart: Reframing self-concepts

» 00:10:58 Lyssa deHart: Reframing life

» 00:11:02 Lyssa deHart: Givingpermission;Igivemyselfpermission

As we begin the coaching session with the client, we are listening for powerful words, ideas, values, and beliefs, capturing what is important to the client so that they can reflect on their own words. These words have meaning to the client. I will also throw in words that I intuit or hear that seem important or that reflect something that appears as the client is speaking.

Coach: What does that mean? Being more of oneself?

Client: Drawing from my personal experience and what I observe in my clients, there can often be significant barriers between how we feel when we are alone and how we express ourselves in the world. The more aligned we are with ourselves, the easier it becomes to go out and express ourselves because we feel more comfortable taking a stand for ourselves. Though it's important to clarify that taking a stand for yourself doesn't necessarily mean being forceful. It's more about allowing yourself to just be you.

Notes in the chat box:

» 00:11:45   Lyssa deHart: Barriers between your self-experience and the external   experience

» 00:11:50   Lyssa deHart: I am more aligned

» 00:11:57   Lyssa deHart: Taking a stand for yourself; I take a stand for myself

» 00:12:18   Lyssa deHart: Allowing of being yourself

Our clients often speak externally about what they want for others. Part of this process is to invite the "I" into the statements in the present tense: "I give myself permission," "I am more aligned," "I take a stand for myself." These ideas show up in my notes. In this way, the client and I are working to develop a future state, but you want to write it as a present state experience. The goal is that the client owns the experience they want. This is difficult for people to verbalize for a myriad of reasons: fear, not wanting to seem big-headed, and so on. Yet with a written goal—for example, "I want to feel XYZ somewhere in the future"—they must continue to strive for that. It may feel unattainable. "I am grounded" is a present state statement. There is nothing in the way. They are grounded now.

Coach: When you think of yourself, who is the being you are wanting to allow?

Client: That's a really good question. To me, there is a feeling experience of one that's stepping into awe.

Coach: That's beautiful—stepping into awe. So is there anything that goes with this stepping into awe? What is the felt experience of stepping into awe? Is there any more that's important to name here?

Client: So that stepping into part is the recognition that you're part of everything, and therefore you matter. And that however you express yourself, it matters. It has that ripple effect to everything, which is where that frequency comes in, right? We constantly affect each other all the time, and we may not even know how much we do so. The more of that highest possible vibration that each person can bring, the more we create a world that, in my hope and vision, is kind.

Notes in the chat box:

» 00:12:52   Lyssa deHart: Stepping into awe

» 00:13:25   Lyssa deHart: A part of everything

» 00:13:28   Lyssa deHart: You matter

» 00:13:40   Lyssa deHart: How you express yourself is a ripple

» 00:14:32   Lyssa deHart: The highest possible vibration each person can be, the more impact they'll have on the world positively

We want to listen to the powerful words and concepts the client shares.

Coach: I'm hearing that the more we're able to step into those higher vibrations, the more we are able to . . .

Client: . . . impact the world positively.

Coach: I have captured a bunch of things in the chat. Do you want to read them? Or do you want me to read them back to you?

Client: You know, if you could read them back to me, that would be helpful.

Coach: Help to support raising the frequency of the planet. Empowered choice. Reframing self-concepts. Reframing life. Giving permission. Being more than themselves. Barriers between your self-experience and the external experience. More aligned. Taking a stand for yourself. Allowing of being yourself. Stepping into awe. You are a part of everything. How you express yourself is a ripple. The highest possible vibration each person can be, the more impact they'll have on the world positively.

What are the things that really drew you in as you heard them reflected back to you?

Client: Definitely the stepping into all. And there was something when you talked about self-expression or the reframing itself. I don't quite remember.

Coach: So being more of themselves, reframing self-concepts, reframing life, the barriers between your self-experience and the external experience, or the external expression. I was just capturing words. Did any of that sound right? Or was there something different?

Client: When you say, "Reframing life," that really resonated with me. I guess I said it.

Coach: May I share something that showed up as you spoke that I thought was really powerful? I don't know if it is important or not, but I'm going to share it.

Client: yes

Coach: You are a ripple.

Client: Yeah. That too.

Coach: Stepping into all, reframing life, you are a ripple.

Client: It's almost a poem, right? It's almost a poem

Coach: As you hear that, is there any piece that's missing? Or is there a way you would want to wordsmith it, where you're really inviting the "I" and the ownership? The outcome of this is that you support others. But this is for you.

Client: I am a ripple. This is not the right wording, but I facilitate reframing life. It's so interesting because you're asking me to think about me. I'm so used to thinking about how I affect others. I'm kind of facilitating or spreading out, which is not about me. So, yeah, I like that. I like that a lot. It brings tears to my eyes.

Coach: What's showing up around that statement for you right now?

Client: I'm going to cry. It acknowledges the beauty. You know, the beauty that's here in the world, and a lot of what we get to deal with on a daily basis is not so beautiful. It's really harsh for a lot of people, and to be part of the whole, and to know that I am part of the whole.

Notes in the chat box:

» 00:17:20   Lyssa deHart: Stepping into awe, reframing life
» 00:17:54   Lyssa deHart: You are a ripple
» 00:19:27   Lyssa deHart: I am a ripple, reframing life, I step into awe.

By playing with the client's words, capturing the ones that seemed important, and giving her time to see what she had shared, she began to develop a goal that touched her heart and had deep meaning. All the issues of how she shows up in life will inevitably appear under the umbrella of "I am a ripple. Reframing life, I step into awe."

It Must Be Meaningful

In *Man's Search for Meaning* (1988), Viktor E. Frankl explores the incredible resilience of individuals who have a strong sense of purpose or meaning in life, even when faced with extreme suffering such as in concentration camps. He argues that those who have a powerful *why* to live can bear almost any *how*. This aligns closely with the concept of supporting the client to name their EGG in the sense that having a deeply ingrained goal or purpose—so deeply ingrained that it affects one's cognitive, emotional, and even physiological state—can provide the resilience, focus, and motivation needed to overcome even the most challenging circumstances that get in the way of living the life purpose.

I find it interesting that given that each of us is a unique amalgamation of character, values, experiences and, ultimately, life purpose, we would use cookie-cutter goals. If you are at a hard yes to do something, to change your life in some epic and meaningful way or even to live in your intention, then you probably need a goal as big and as meaningful as you and your life's purpose.

When the client creates powerful visual language, it has a visceral and experiential meaning for them. It becomes owned. Just like the metaphors we are listening for in our conversations. These EGGs are owned and rich with meaning.

Even the idea of an EGG is metaphorical, for what do eggs represent? Eggs are significant in various mythologies and spiritual traditions, symbolizing new beginnings, purity, fertility, rebirth, and the potential for life. Found in every culture and continent, the egg has always held particular symbolic significance, partly because it is a visual shorthand for new life and unhatched potential (Jackson 2017). The egg is woven into the fabric of many spiritual and mythological traditions, representing everything from the cosmos's birth to the individual's spiritual journey.

When the client creates and then begins to use their EGG to ground themselves in every situation that rocks their world, they can easily determine when they are in or out of alignment with how they want to show up in the world. This goal is the being of the client. When they need to reorient and ground themselves, the goal will be remembered, supporting actions and serving as a compass for the goal of how they want to navigate their life.

That's empowering.

A Caveat to Note-Taking

As a coach, your presence is invaluable to your client. Being fully present means you are actively engaged and attentive to their words, thoughts, and energy. However, note-taking can be a hindrance to this level of presence, as it can distract you from fully connecting with them.

Imagine yourself sitting with your client, pen in hand, scribbling notes as they speak. Although you may be capturing important details, your focus is divided, and you risk missing subtle cues in your client's tone, body language, energy, or facial expressions. These non-verbal cues can reveal volumes about what your client is really feeling or thinking, and without them, you may not be able to offer the most useful question to what they have shared.

That being said, there are times when taking notes can be beneficial for both you and your client. In the first session, as noted in the previous example, it can be helpful to take notes that your client can see. This lets them reflect on what they've shared and to take ownership of their thoughts and feelings. Similarly, if your client is expressing powerful or emotional words, writing them down for their benefit can show that you are listening, and it gives them a tangible way to process their thoughts.

However, discernment is key when it comes to note-taking. It's important to be mindful of when and how often you take notes and to prioritize being fully present with your client over capturing details. Ultimately, the value of being fully present cannot be overstated, as it lays the foundation for a strong and trusting coach-client relationship.

Questions

● How can a grounding statement or goal help individuals in

coaching to stay focused and motivated?

- How might a grounded and embodied goal serve as an over-arching desire that encompasses various aspects of a person's life?

- Why is it important for a client to have a goal that is fully owned and known by them, and how does it contribute to their personal growth and reorientation in challenging situations?

- What learning is showing up for you?

Reading Recommendation

Man's Search for Meaning by Viktor E. Frankl

Chapter 13: Emotions Are Like Road Signs

> " Emotions are not reactions to the world; they are your constructions of the world.
>
> —Lisa Feldman Barrett

The power in listening for emotions is not that a coach needs to explore every emotion with their client but that emotions are openings. They give us and our clients vital information. Because the emotions are coming from the client, the client often has the capacity to explain what they are experiencing.

As a coach, one of the most valuable skills you can have is your ability to truly listen to your clients. But it's not just about hearing what they're saying; it's about picking up on the emotional language they're using and getting curious about what that means to them regarding their experiences, thoughts, feelings, and behaviors. Ultimately, to be heard is fundamental to being coached and is a rare gift for most of us.

Returning to the research of Lisa Feldman Barrett (2020), she notes that emotions are not fixed states that we experience but rather are constructed by our brains based on a complex web of past experiences, social and cultural influences, and physical sensations. This means that the emotional language we use—the words we choose to describe how we feel—can provide powerful clues about the deeper beliefs and experiences that underlie our emotions. Because these constructs are often complex, they are usually shared in the form of metaphorical language.

By tuning in to the emotion and then inviting the visual language, you can help the client gain a deeper understanding of their emotions and what's driving them. For example, when the client comes to the session, you can do the following:

Coach: What is coming to the surface for you for coaching today?

Client: I'm not feeling great emotionally. I feel crappy, like I'm a bad person and selfish. Despite this, I've been thinking a lot about our last session, where we discussed my life vision. It's got me reflecting on what I really want out of life, both on a personal and a professional level, and what changes I need to make.

            I have a lot of questions on my mind. Specifically, I'm questioning how much time Bob and I are spending together. I'm also wondering if maybe I need to take a break from being in a relationship altogether right now.

Coach: Okay. I'm hearing multiple threads. Is there one that you would like to focus on for this conversation?

Client: I don't know. I'm just . . . I don't . . . You know, it just feels confusing, so . . .

Coach: May I ask if you could paint a picture of the confusion? What is the confusion?

Client: It looks like a tangled mess of grayish-black strings and fuzz, with no bright light or blue sky around it. The entire image is knotted and messy, and it feels as if no light is coming through. It's all just a grayish-black vision.

Coach: What would you like to do with that messy, knotted, tangled, fuzzy vision?

Client: I would like to untangle it. I would like to find some clarity. You know, I want clarity. I would like to find the threads that come through that are on the other side that are light.

Coach: What would it look like on the untangled light side?

Client: There would be no fuzz. All the threads would be illuminated, light and bright, and it would feel lighter. It would feel freeing, and maybe the threads might still have some bend to them, but they're not a knotted mess.

Coach: That is a beautiful image to move toward. What would be the first step in moving toward that vision of the illuminated threads?

"It looks like a tangled mess of grayish-black strings and fuzz, with no bright light or blue sky around it. The entire image is knotted and messy, and it feels as if no light is coming through. It's all just a grayish-black vision." This is the metaphorical imagery of the emotion of confusion. In this case, confusion doesn't feel light and freeing; it is perceived as heavy and tangled. An exploration of confusion is going to take the client in circles and probably to a very heavy place while an exploration of the illuminated threads is probably going to take us forward into a lighter place.

Remember source and target as you think about this.

Source: Concrete Concept	Target: Abstract Concept
Tangled mess of strings and fuzz	Confusion

Again, the client had said, "Confusion," but by painting the picture of her emotions, we now have a safe way to explore the emotion of confusion without going in circles. A coach might ask, "What does confusion feel like?" But this is a less than useful question, as it takes the client down the road of the distress they are feeling. Instead, by giving imagery to the powerful emotion, we support the client in the clarity of distance. It's not confusion; it's a tangled ball of strings and fuzz. And we know where we are heading—toward the illuminated threads—which feel freeing and lighter.

Powerful Emotions

It might be the experience of powerlessness, a feeling of being under-valued, or something else entirely. By exploring the nuances of the client's emotional language, you can help them uncover the underly-ing important awareness that their emotions are sharing with them so that they can gain new insights into what's really going on.

"I want to explore work-life balance. I'm feeling stressed all the time." This is a pretty typical client request. Although it's useful to explore the experience that goes with feeling stressed, I would rather do so through the lens of a metaphor. "If you were to describe the stress, what does it look like to you?" "A heavy cloud," "a pressure cooker," "bogged down," or "I'm dogpaddling in circles." The client creates these idea containers to express emotion. They are also not as overwhelming as being stressed. They give both coach and client a way to explore that isn't using the word stress repeatedly. Instead, we ask, "What needs to happen with the heavy cloud by the end of our session?" or "If you weren't dogpaddling in circles, what would you rather be doing?"

These questions also ask about outcome expectations. The an-swer to that last question could be, "Sitting on the pier looking out over calm water." If you consider this, you can hear the emotional shift that is happening. The coach now has a hypothesis of a direction from the client to test. "Is that what would be useful today? Moving from dogpaddling in circles to sitting on a pier looking out over calm water?"

Threat to Safety Continuum

I operate on the idea that all emotions fall on a spectrum from safety to threat. When we feel safe, we feel positive emotions. When we feel threatened, negative emotions surface. The threat could be to our person, ideas, opinions, sense of self, values, or deeply held beliefs. Threats typically generate a defensive response, and those responses can be directed at ourselves or toward others. Being curious about all emotions is fundamental to having self-awareness, experiencing aha moments and, ultimately, making new, purposeful choices.

Let's consider a scenario that the client brings this to coaching:

Client: I'm feeling stressed today because I have so many choices about what to get done or which project to complete. The overload of options leaves me feeling confused and bogged down, so I end up doing nothing at all.

We hear "stressed," and hopefully we also hear "overload of options" and "bogged down." We can use these metaphors as a doorway to the underlying concerns the client is wrangling with.

Outside In

When we ask questions that shift our client's attention out of the feelings and into the situation, we miss an opportunity to dive inward and support emerging wisdom. This approach is outside-in coaching. Outside-in questions often support the situation rather than move toward maximizing insights and self-awareness.

Questions that shift the conversation outside in tend to focus on the situation:

- How do you organize your day?
- What are all your options?
- What do you need to get done?
- Has there ever been a time in your life when it was easier to make choices?

These aren't bad questions; depending on your timing,

some of them might be useful. When asked too early in the inquiry, though, these questions shift attention from exploring the emotional narrative. Because all clients and conversations are unique, we might eventually get to the underlying issue. Yet what would open up your client's curiosity more immediately?

Emotional intelligence involves not only being comfortable with one's own emotions and the emotions of others but also understanding and managing them effectively. If we pass over our clients emotions, we may unwittingly communicate that they are too messy, or that they aren't important, or that we are uncomfortable with what appeared in the space. Even emotions like stress can send coaches running to "fix" the feeling with solutions like exercises and lists. That's fine, but without your willingness to dig below the surface, your clients don't have the opportunity to understand themselves with greater clarity.

Road Signs

What if we shift our relationship to emotions and see them as road signs? Driving down the road, you see many signs like NO RIGHT ON RED, SCHOOL CROSSING, or SPEED LIMIT 45. These signs signal something useful, just as emotions tell us useful information. They are a doorway into deepening awareness.

Emotions don't evaporate. We may squelch or soothe them for a time, but they continue to bubble each time we feel them in a similar situation. Because they are constructed from experience, similar experiences evoke similar emotions. This is partly why it's useful to explore what is showing up when a client is experiencing an emotion in coaching. What does it tell the client about what is important here? What other things do you notice that are similar to this emotional experience?

Remember, if your clients had solved the deeper experience of particular feelings, they wouldn't bring the topic to a coaching session. And if they do bring the emotion to the session, it is because they are ready to explore it a bit, and they have trust that you can hold the space for inquiry.

Clients get attached to situations that cause negative emotions. It's common to find yourself listening to the surface stories of who did what to whom. Take the time to listen for the buried treasure. Ask questions that explore the client's emotional waters. There is an assumption of trust and safety when the deeper meaningful issues come to the surface; it's an opportunity to explore below the waterline.

Inside Out

Let's reexamine the earlier scenario of a client who says, "I'm feeling stressed today because I have so many choices about what to get done or which project to complete. The overload of options leaves me feeling confused and bogged down, so I end up doing nothing at all."

Questions that invite the client to explore the emotion, and not the situation, ultimately give them the internal tools to navigate the same or similar feelings the next time they pop up.

Questions that invite inside-out exploration include the following:

- I'm hearing "overload of options" and "bogged down." What, if anything, might be important to explore in there?
- If we were to fully explore the overload of options, what would be different for you at the end of the conversation?
- What is the experience you have when you're not bogged down?
- I am hearing "bogged down" and "ending up doing nothing at all." What is the first place we need to explore to move towards taking action?

These types of questions support clients by acknowledging that we heard the stress and invite them to consider what they would prefer instead, without getting into the swirl of the surface story. Metaphors help us here, as the client has already shared them, and their brain is lit up with what those idea containers mean to them.

By diving into conscious curiosity surrounding metaphorical emotions, you offer your clients a powerful gift. Feelings are useful, not scary. Clients can use their inquiry and awareness to examine situations and expand their internal wisdom. And that, my friend, is a forever tool.

Questions

- What shows up as you consider how you might explore emotions in the context of supporting a client to develop deeper awareness?

- What is the significance of viewing emotions as road signs and using them as a doorway to deeper awareness and personal growth?

- How can metaphors and visual language enhance the understanding of clients' emotions and experiences?

- What stands out for your learning from this chapter?

Reading Recommendation

How Emotions Are Made: The Secret Life of the Brain by Lisa Feldman Barrett

Chapter 14: Culturally Competent Coaching

" Psychological Safety is a belief that the context is safe for interpersonal risk-taking—that speaking up with ideas, questions, concerns, or mistakes will be welcomed and valued even when I'm wrong. It's a sense of permission for candor.

—Amy Edmondson, *The Fearless Organization*

If there are 8.1 billion people on the planet, then there are probably 32 billion cultural identities. Most of us belong to or identify with multiple cultures. We may identify by religious background, cultural identity, color, location, gender, experience, education, values, or all of the above. Each of us comes from a frame of reference based entirely on a unique personal lens made of the elements we most identify with and then we tend to assume that those lenses are the same for our clients. If I walked through the world assuming that every other person shared my perspective, experiences, or influences, I would be missing an opportunity to step into curiosity and honor that my clients are most likely a complex system of unique perspectives, experiences, and influences.

In this chapter, we'll look at examples of coaching with cultural competence and acknowledge that this is the work of a lifetime for most of us. Culturally competent coaching means creating radical trust with our clients and expanding our courage in how we are being with others so that we are not only willing to hear experiences through different perspectives but also willing to invite those different perspectives. From a cultural lens, courage is not just in showing up; it's in being willing to listen to another person's experience deeply. It's about letting go of our ideas of rightness, wrongness, or meaning and turning fully to our clients to make their own meaning based on their frames of reference. It's also about being compassionate with ourselves on the journey as we learn to be in an open and beginner's mind with all the variety of people with whom we work.

Radical Trust Takes Radical Courage

What it takes to be culturally competent is an interesting thing. I think cultural competency is one of the most courageous acts, in part because we must find ways to open ourselves to the reality that we may step in it at some point. And we must be willing to own, not that we intended to impact another person negatively, but that we did impact another person in a way we never intended.

With all my clients, I start by setting agreements regarding how we will handle the possible or inevitable differences that will appear as we get to know one another. Transparently, I am a white woman raised in the United States. I have a life experience that has been influenced by how others in the world see me and, conversely, how I see the world. In all honesty, I have experienced cultural differences even with people who look just like me, as everyone in the world will have had often vastly different experiences. As coaches and as human beings, it benefits us to make few, if any, assumptions about other people. It is important to acknowledge these differences, especially in a coaching relationship, where trust is fundamental to how we create a trusted space to explore tender parts of people.

It is one thing in the agreement-setting process to say to your client, "Please, if I say or do something that lands poorly with you, let me know." It is quite different when a client takes you up on this offer and tells you, "Hey, that's not working." It takes an emotional equilibrium to be okay with being called out and also being okay with not being perfect and having everyone like you, all the time, about everything. A coach can quickly start feeling judged and shamed just as fast as any of their clients. It takes radical courage to breathe into a client being upset with us and still keep our curiosity and willingness to hear that person's perspective.

Radical courage is also needed as we work on our self-awareness. Self-awareness of our biases is crucial to our capacity to be in the space of curiosity and openness to another viewpoint when we feel we may be being misunderstood or told that we unintentionally hurt another person. Understanding what biases you have and how they appear and are demonstrated takes a willingness to look into our own shadows.

What does it take for you to look inside yourself at the stuff that may be unconsciously nestling in the dark?

Sapir-Whorf Principle

Edward Sapir and his pupil Benjamin Lee Whorf hypothesized that language influences thought rather than the reverse. They presented the principle of linguistic relativity not as a hypothesis but as a discovery from linguistic analysis, stating that grammar is not just a tool for expression but actively shapes ideas and thought processes. Fundamentally, people of different cultures think differently because of their language differences (Holmes 2001, pp. 14,562–14,569).

If we then do a quick mash-up with the influence of metaphors on thought and language referencing Lakoff's claim that our daily thinking and actions are deeply embedded in metaphor, this syncs with the Sapir-Whorf hypothesis. The Sapir-Whorf hypothesis, also known as linguistic relativity, posits that the structure of a language affects its speaker's cognition and behavior. In the context of metaphors, this hypothesis suggests that the metaphors prevalent in a language can shape the thoughts and actions of its speakers. "You cross a river by feeling the stones" is similar yet demonstrates a different context than something like, "I need to stay in my lane so I can get where I am going."

According to Lakoff and Johnson (1980), our everyday thoughts and actions are steeped in metaphor, indicating that our conceptual system is largely metaphorical in nature. This idea aligns with the Sapir-Whorf hypothesis by implying that our cognition—how we think, reason, and perceive the world—is influenced by the metaphors that are embedded in our language. If our thought processes are metaphorical and our language shapes thought, then the metaphors we use can profoundly affect how we experience the world.

The concept of metaphorical framing, as discussed, involves recognizing that metaphors shape people's perception and understanding of a situation. For instance, a client describes an office shake-up as a "dumpster fire." They have framed the situation in a way that impacts the insight and attitude of not only the client but also of the coach, influencing how the listener perceives the experience the client is having. This highlights the importance of testing our hypothesis that things at the office sound alarming. As the listener, we might be 100 percent correct, or maybe the client is adding levity to the conversation by using the metaphor hyperbolically.

The 2013 study "Natural Language Metaphors Covertly Influence Reasoning" by Thibodeau and Boroditsky revealed that metaphors can greatly impact people's perspectives and the solutions they suggest for problems, such as crime. The researchers found that metaphors framing crime as a "virus" led participants to consider systemic solutions, like addressing poverty or improving education. Conversely, metaphors that depicted crime as a "beast" prompted participants to favor punitive measures, such as more aggressive law enforcement and stricter penalties for criminals. Interestingly, these effects on reasoning persisted even when participants could not recall the specific metaphors of "virus" or "beast," indicating that metaphorical language can subtly but powerfully shape thought processes and decision-making (Thibodeau & Boroditsky, 2013). This underscores the significant influence of metaphorical language on how individuals conceptualize and approach societal issues.

The Sapir-Whorf hypothesis in relation to metaphors underscores the potential power of language to shape our reality. If our conceptual systems are metaphorical, as Lakoff and Johnson argue, then we are reminded that the metaphors we use are not merely linguistic flourishes but tools that can structure our worldview, the society we live in, and the experience we are having.

In a recent coaching conversation, my client was upset that "all the balls . . . were being dropped, and I don't know what to do." By the end of the conversation, their language was, "It's like the sun is breaking through the clouds." This demonstrates two very different mindsets from beginning to end of the coaching call. The movement from one metaphor to the other demonstrates the shift in the client's experience of their situation and ends the call with a more empowered position. This underscores the importance of being aware of the metaphors that we and our clients use, as they can reflect and influence our worldviews and actions. Using the metaphors that our clients share demonstrates respect for these nuanced differences.

How Metaphors Invite Cultural Competency

In weaving the threads of cultural competence throughout our coaching conversations, metaphors emerge as a uniquely powerful tool. It's a way of engaging with our clients that requires us to inhabit a space of profound listening, a presence of being with, where we honor the words and visions springing directly from the client's mind and world.

Think of it as joining a dance with a rhythm set by the client where we, as coaches, follow their lead. This dance is not choreographed by our own assumptions or cultural lenses. Instead, we remain in a state of deep, open curiosity, eager to understand and explore the rich landscape of their experiences.

As we harness metaphors that resonate with the client, we're doing more than just listening—we're demonstrating that we see, hear, and value their unique perspective. We're acknowledging that their cultural context, their stories, and their imagery are the materials from which solutions and growth can be co-created.

Imagine a client who describes their challenge as "feeling like I'm constantly swimming against the tide." If we jump in with our own interpretations or solutions, we're imposing our narrative upon theirs. However, if we stay inquisitive, asking what this tide looks like, how it feels, and what swimming with the tide might allow for them, we invite a depth of understanding. This isn't just about clarifying the metaphor; it's about immersing ourselves in their cultural waters, learning to swim alongside them rather than directing them to our shore—or shouting out solutions from the beach.

By valuing and using the metaphors that organically arise from our clients, we affirm their expertise in their own lives. We're not assuming anything; we're discovering, with respectful wonder, the world they navigate every day. This approach not only fosters a culturally competent coaching relationship but also empowers clients, showing them that their voice, culture, and internal imagery are the compass by which we'll journey together toward their goals.

A Short Cautionary Tale

I was observing a coaching fishbowl in a class, and as the coach and client were developing the agreement, the coach asked the client something to the effect of the following: "What would be different at the end of the conversation that would make it most useful?" Great question.

Client: I would have enlightenment.

Coach: Enlightenment. That's a really big word.

This is such a subtle bias, but at this point, the client started backtracking, lost focus, and the conversation lost trust. There was an implicit and frankly explicit judgment about the client regarding their desire to have enlightenment. Yet as an observer of the conversation, I saw that the client didn't mean enlightenment as in a Buddha sitting on a lotus blossom. Rather, they wanted to shine a light on the issue.

The coach's frame of reference demonstrated bias and shut down the curiosity needed to explore meaning, which would involve letting go of our own meaning and asking questions such as, "When you say, 'Enlightenment,' how would you know you were there?"

This type of coaching situation happens all the time. With our lenses fixed firmly to our faces, we all naturally see the world from our own frame of reference. Unless we intentionally get curious and investigate our filters, we will stay unconscious of how our biases, beliefs, ideas of rightness and wrongness, and stories about how things must be done or not done may unintentionally get dumped on others.

Anytime we get into a space of assuming, knowing, or certitude, we are at risk of stepping outside of cultural competence. Given that many different cultures exist, we can give a lot of space to ask questions, explore meaning, and learn with our clients.

Implicit Bias

I highly recommend Harvard's ongoing research program, Project Implicit (see www.projectimplicit.net). Annually, I go there to take an implicit bias test or five. When I first found Project Implicit, I took a test and discovered that I had, around the year 2000, a very strong bias toward men in leadership positions. I would have laughed if you had asked me if I was biased toward men as leaders. I was a strong, independent, young woman. I had a career, and I didn't see men as inherently better at leading than women. As a young person, I didn't inherently respect many people, but those I did respect were often female. I liked men; I worked for the military and was surrounded by men. I was married to a man and I loved my cutie—still do—but even our relationship was built on ideas of partnership.

Yet there it was; the way and speed in which I responded to men and words of power and women and words of power showed that hidden in my brain was a bias toward men. This was eye-opening and crucial to how I functioned in my job. I didn't need to swing hard in the opposite direction; I did, however, need to remain conscious of my awareness to ensure I was not letting my bias make unconscious decisions for me.

I recently took the test again, and the bias toward men is still there. It's a slight bias now instead of a strong one, but I still have it, even with twenty years of conscious understanding. It's very difficult to completely shift a bias when your culture reconfirms the rightness of it daily.

Now consider if you are a person of color, or you belong to a religion that isn't mainstream in your community, or you don't fit the typical ideas of gender or sexuality. You live in a larger system that doesn't reflect you. And you are, most likely, having experiences that someone in the mainstream may have no experience with at all.

When I was in graduate school, there was a lesbian couple who knew I had a photography background. They were getting married and asked if I could take some photos of them. If you had asked me in that moment my thoughts, I would have told you that I had many LGBTQ friends and that I thought finding love was more important than whom you found love with. And so, I said, "Yes, absolutely. I am happy to take the photos."

Then my work began. I had doubts; I was uncomfortable. Should I take a photo of them kissing? What the heck was I going to do? All this unconscious baggage about marriage, roles, man/woman, my comfort level with differences, cultural norms, and what people would think about me came bubbling to the surface. I remember lying down on the floor, breathing into it, and getting curious. This process required me to be radically curious and conscious of myself and my unconscious baggage.

After I had sorted through my beliefs and biases, I shared with my friends that I had gotten into a bit of a twist about the photos and that it had surprised me that the biases were even lurking below the surface. I wanted them to know that I was thoroughly excited to take the photos. Then it was their turn: "Do you think we should take photos of us kissing? Is that too much?" They too lived in a larger cultural environment that did not reflect what was available to them, and their implicit bias against their relationship showed up. Ultimately, we had some eye-opening conversations and took some awesome photos, with all of us aligned with what we were doing and what they wanted.

Courage

If you have a brain, you're biased. Yet we often think this applies to other people and not to us. Especially when it comes to biases that might unintentionally harm others. We say to ourselves, "We're nice people; we wouldn't intentionally hurt another person." Yet it's this lack of self-awareness that is the thing that leads us to unintentionally harm others. Then, when we are fact-checked on something we said or did, it leads us to get defensive and hurt them again.

Courage is not just in showing up; it's in hearing another person's experience and then being willing to let go of attachment to the idea that "That's not me! I'm not a hurtful person!" and instead bravely show up in a more useful manner.

In part, this bravery comes from awareness of self and others. This is explored in the article "Buried Prejudice: The Bigot in Your Brain" (Carpenter 2008). The article speaks to the fundamental truth that everyone possesses implicit biases, subtly sculpted by societal and cultural conditioning. (Remember, if you have a brain, you're biased.) This concept is especially crucial for coaches to recognize, as it illuminates their potential to unknowingly harbor both positive and negative biases toward clients. Moreover, these implicit biases can imperceptibly affect a coach's judgment, questioning approach, and interactions with clients. By acknowledging this, coaches can actively work toward minimizing these biases and their impacts, creating a more neutral or clean way of holding space in coaching.

One of the most effective ways to counteract these subconscious prejudices is through self-awareness. Understanding that biases exist and being mindful of their potential influence in our professional interactions enables us to make our coaching practices more equitable and effective. It prompts us to question our automatic assumptions or responses, keeping us alert to the pitfalls of how our brain is wired.

This article also highlights that overcoming our buried prejudices isn't a one-time task but rather a constant journey of learning, reflection, and adaptation. This insight is of great significance for coaches striving for cultural competency, underlining the need for continuous growth and adaptation.

Psychological Safety

Harvard Business School professor Amy Edmondson delved deep into the dynamics of teamwork and interpersonal relationships at work. She defined psychological safety as the belief that one will not be punished or humiliated for speaking up with ideas, questions, concerns, or mistakes. In her extensive research, Edmondson (2018) illuminated how team members were more likely to share information, innovate, and address mistakes constructively in environments where psychological safety thrived. Without this foundation, fear could stifle the exchange of ideas and limit the potential for growth. Psychological safety is not just about fostering comfort but about nurturing an environment where risk-taking is allowed and encouraged. Her studies provided a blueprint for organizations and teams aspiring to achieve cohesion and excellence.

Understanding psychological safety is one thing and integrating it into our daily practices is another. As coaches, mentors, and leaders, we must ask ourselves: Are we creating environments that encourage open dialogue and acceptance? I had one session where my attachment to an idea stopped me from hearing my clients' negative experience. My bias of how something was "supposed" to sound made me attached to something ridiculous. My client called me out on it, but each time I recall that coaching session, I'm reminded of how easy it is to either build or erode the safety of our conversations.

Coaches have a lot to explore, regardless of working in organizations or with individuals. Edmondson's work is not just a theoretical construct but a lived experience, a guiding principle that challenges us all to be more intentional in fostering spaces where everyone feels safe to speak, disagree, make mistakes, and ultimately learn and grow.

Circling Back to Metaphors

If I am using powerful words and images to create meaning for myself, a coach who listens and, even more importantly, hears me, is going to leave me feeling seen. And I cannot say this enough: being seen and heard is fundamental to our experience in coaching. It is also a rare gift that a coach gives their client.

A quick reminder: people may use metaphors unconsciously but not unintentionally.

When we join in their worldview and hear the words that resonate with their internal landscape, we demonstrate full partnering with our clients.

Let's explore some examples.

Example 1

Client: What is most evident to me today is that I sometimes have so many obligations. Despite being organized, I often find myself overwhelmed by all the demands on how to spend my time. Instead of focusing on completing a project, I end up spinning my wheels. I just feel loaded down. I get so busy with details that I don't feel like I accomplish much. How do I balance all that I need to do so that I complete my work? How do I balance everything to get the most out of every day instead of just giving up, feeling bogged down by it all?

In what the client offered, we hear "spinning my wheels," "loaded down," "balance," and "bogged down." These all point to a target, a test of the hypothesis—overwhelm. If, as the coach, we reflect the client's language, we can't help but demonstrate competency in their cultural and internal framework. The language that the client is using is important to them. There are many ways to ask the questions that invite the client forward. I call them choice points.

- Choice point: I want to acknowledge that I heard "spinning my wheels," "bogged down," and "balance." What of these, if anything, is showing up as important to look at in coaching today?

- Choice point: I heard "spinning my wheels," "loaded down," and "balance." When you hear those reflected back, what would be important for us to explore?

- Choice point: If you no longer felt your wheels spinning and being bogged down, what would be different for you?

There are infinite choice points for the coach. In each of these, the coach is demonstrating stepping into the world of the client through the metaphorical language.

Example 2

Client: I have an upcoming interview, and I'm feeling a mix of excitement, nervousness, and hope. Today, I want to discuss how I can cultivate the right mindset to excel in this interview and present my best self. How can I prepare mentally so that I don't enter the interview overly nervous or end up rambling?

Here is another example of the client sharing their language and perspective. They have offered their emotional state, "a mix of excitement, nervousness, and hope," as well as the desire to "cultivate the right mindset" so that they don't "end up rambling." These all give us clues around which to test meaning.

- Choice point: If you get the mix right, what mix might cultivate the right mindset to present your best self?

- Choice point: What helps you to cultivate the right mindset when you're feeling the mix of excitement, nervousness, and hope?

- Choice point: What is the connection between cultivating

the right mindset and not ending up rambling?

Again, by using the client's vernacular and metaphors, we reduce cognitive load. Their mind is already open to these words; they feel seen and heard, and we can leverage the metaphors to invite them to guide us through what is important to them.

Transactional Analysis Framework

Understanding the roles of parent/expert, adult/equal, and child/novice from a transactional analysis (TA) framework is profoundly insightful for a professional coach striving for cultural competency. To begin with, this framework makes coaches acutely aware of power dynamics (Bright 2018).

When a coach assumes the parent/expert role, they may risk being patronizing or overly authoritative. This can be especially problematic when engaging with individuals from cultures that highly value deference to authority or, on the flip side, prefer egalitarian interactions. In contrast, the child/novice stance lets the coach place the client in the expert position. This positioning enables the coach to support the client to glean self-awareness and insights while staying in the client's cultural and metaphorical context.

Many people come to coaching thinking that the coach is the expert—in marketing, in career changes, in parenting, in writing, in executive presence, in leadership, in confidence, in whatever your area of expertise. Many of us have grown up in families where the parents or teachers tell us what to do, with the expectation that we will do it. From a TA perspective, this typically leads to two types of responses: the accommodating child (I'll do what you say) or the rebellious child (No! No! No!).

Inherent in this description is a reminder that coaching is a co-creative process between two adults, two peers, two equals, both bringing themselves fully to the conversation. If, as a coach, we get into the habit of telling our clients what they *should* do, *should* think about, *should* explore, or *should* fix in their situations, we take their power. First, that's a lot of *should*'ing on people, and second, what sort of hubris is it to think that any of us can solve another person's relationship to their stories and life? That is the work of each of us for ourselves.

Listening deeply, being curious about a client's use of words, and having an open mindset are integral to this framework. As the coach adopts the adult/equal and/or the child/novice role, there is freedom in not knowing, in not being the expert, and it has the added benefit of empowering clients.

TA invites coaches to be inquisitive, posing questions and endeavoring to understand a client's unique identity, experiences, and perspectives without making hasty judgments. This self-awareness also enhances the coach's capacity for empathy, which helps the coach discern the underlying emotions and motivations, inviting curiosity, and ultimately better resonating with their clients.

When we consciously choose to be the novice and let our client be the expert, we practice true cultural competence. It's a journey through their internal landscape, using their metaphors, powerful beliefs, and somatic responses to notice where they lead and then follow. Understanding that our expectations and directions shouldn't overshadow our clients' experiences is crucial. It's a common misconception that cultural competence is only about differences in color or nationality. We could be the same color, the same culture, but if we impose our own perceptions, opinions, limits, beliefs, or values on another person, we are being culturally incompetent in that moment.

There's a certain beauty in this role reversal, this dance of power dynamics. We move away from a transactional analysis perspective of parent/expert to the client's child/novice dynamic. Instead, we adopt a childlike wonder; we become the partner, the equal and, at times, the novice to their expertise, letting the client guide us.

How Partnership Can Look

I was working with a Chinese client several years ago, and she brought forward a metaphor I never could have come up with. But by embracing her language and lens, the conversation became helpful as a map that supported her to move forward.

Coach: What is showing up for today's conversation?

Client: I want to write a book, but I am having trouble with actually writing. I am overwhelmed and can't see the steps I need to take to make words appear on the page. This has been going on for a while, and I am really frustrated with myself.

Coach: As you said that, I saw a path opening up in front of us. What do you see?

Client: No, no. In China, we say, "You cross a river by feeling the stones."

Coach: That may be one of the most beautiful metaphors I have ever heard. Is that what we are doing today— crossing a river?

Client: Yes. I want to cross this river of confusion and frustration [laughter].

Coach: What are we crossing toward?

Client: Clarity. I will have more understanding of what I need to do.

Coach: Which is the first stone we need to feel to cross toward clarity?

In a nutshell, cultural competency is the ability to understand, appreciate, and interact effectively with people from diverse cultures, backgrounds, and beliefs. As a coach, honoring the client's cultural lens, adopting their visual language, and moving alongside them demonstrates partnering and interacting effectively. As we stay open, flexible, and client-centered, we invite the client to determine how their brain needs to explore the current issue they are navigating.

Again, looking at the previous example, the coach is holding lightly to the idea container that showed up for them—the path—and instead moved into the world the client was creating, crossing the river by feeling the stones.

If cultural competence is a dance, then let your clients lead. As we embrace this stance, we allow space for their stories, cultures, and realities, thereby honoring their individuality. That, for me, is the essence of cultural competence in coaching.

Questions

- How can our personal lenses and cultural backgrounds influence our coaching approach?

- How do you see metaphors meeting cultural competency?

- How might you shift from expert to equal or novice in your coaching conversations?

Recommended Reading

Your Unique Cultural Lens: A Guide to Cultural Competence by Enrique J. Zaldivar

The Fearless Organization: Creating Psychological Safety in the Workplace for Learning, Innovation, and Growth by Amy Edmondson

Chapter 15: Playful Coaching

" Life isn't divided into genres. It's a horrifying, romantic, tragic, comical, science-fiction cowboy detective novel. You know, with a bit of pornography if you're lucky.

—Alan Moore

One of the hallmarks of good coaching is that we are having important, deep, meaningful conversations. I would add that to have deep, meaningful conversations, even about painful, challenging, or tender topics, the capacity to access humor and playfulness increases the client's capacity to explore themes and develop creative solutions for their situations.

A boatload of research shows the correlation between humor and the reduction of stress hormones. From the simple fight, flight, freeze, and freak-out model, we know that stress, even existential stress from existential threats, has the capacity to shut down a brain in seconds. Basically, anything that moves us from our steady state or homeostasis can activate a stress response (Cannon 1963). These threats flood our brains with cortisol, norepinephrine, adrenaline, and dopamine (Arnsten et al. 2012).

When we laugh, our brain releases endorphins, natural mood boosters that can help reduce stress and anxiety (Robinson et al. 2023). This can be especially important during coaching sessions, as clients may explore challenging, painful, stressful, and/or emotional issues. By incorporating humor and playfulness, coaches can help their clients feel more relaxed and at ease, making it easier for them to engage with the coaching process and explore new ideas.

In addition, laughter has been shown to increase creativity by opening up the mind to new possibilities. When we are in a positive state of mind, we are more likely to be receptive to new ideas and approaches and more willing to take risks and try new things. By incorporating playfulness into coaching sessions, coaches can help spark their clients' creativity and encourage them to think outside the box.

When you are coaching your client and their brain is alight with insights, ideas, and creative flow, not only is the client having fun exploring their topic but so is the coach. I believe that metaphors give us the space needed to delve into serious topics from the lens of joyful or humorous exploration. A brain that feels safe is also a wonder of creativity while a brain that feels any level of threat is going to circle the wagons and become protective. Fear and the desire to self-protect are not the spaces that invite playfulness and humor.

Fundamentally, play is an essential activity that helps us develop a range of skills necessary for life. Whether we're navigating social interactions, solving complex problems, or expressing our creativity, inviting it into your coaching offers your clients a safe space to explore, practice, and refine their understanding of their own self. It's not just about having fun; it's a critical part of how we can safely develop and grow.

The Science of Laughter's Affect on the Brain

The more I work in this field, the more I believe that every thought and experience we have is run through the filter of safety to threat. I talked about this earlier as we explored how you make meaning. I mention this continuum of safety to threat again here because it is, dare I say, impossible to truly laugh and feel threatened at the same time. True laughter and humor help shift the brain from the fear state and invite a more open and receptive mind to play.

Not only is laughter good medicine, but multiple studies have also demonstrated that people who laugh live longer, handle stress better, feel less pain, and have stronger immune systems (Robinson et al. 2023).

One of the most well-documented effects of humor on the brain is its ability to reduce stress. When we laugh, our body releases a cascade of neurotransmitters, including dopamine, serotonin, and endorphins, that counteract the effects of stress hormones like cortisol. This can lead to a sense of relaxation and a reduction in anxiety, which can be particularly helpful for people who are dealing with chronic stress or other mental health challenges.

In addition to its stress-reducing properties, humor has been shown to improve mood and increase happiness. One study found that even anticipating a humorous event, like watching a funny movie, can increase positive emotions and reduce negative ones. Because humor is often a social activity, it can also lead to increased social connection and feelings of belonging, which can be important for overall mental health and well-being (American Psychological Society 2008).

But the benefits of humor on the brain go beyond just mood and stress reduction. Researchers have found that humor can also have positive effects on cognitive function, including memory, creativity, and problem-solving. For example, one study by Mengke Wang and Zengzhao Chen (2022) found that participants who watched a funny video before taking a memory test performed better than those who didn't watch anything. Another study found that humor can stimulate creative thinking and problem-solving by reducing mental rigidity and increasing the ability to think outside the box (Wang and Chen 2022).

With metaphors, the potential is there that we might be able to explore emotionally charged topics with humor and grace. This doesn't mean that we use humor to try to make the client laugh. Rather, we learn to discern the nuances and invitations that the client gives the conversation and leverage that by joyfully embracing it as it shows up and invite the client to embrace it as well.

From Frozen to Peaceful

In this demonstration, the client brings a very painful subject to coaching. Yet, through metaphor and humor, the client can clarify the direction forward, from the state of feeling frozen toward feeling peaceful. This is from a twenty-three-minute coaching session.

Coach: I know we don't have very much time, but I want to say thank you for being willing to show up and play with me today. Do you need anything to bring the curtains down on this so that it really is just you and I together?

Client: I think I just did it. I pinned your video so that I see you, and I'm going to pretend we are in a good space because I have a real topic [laughter].

Coach: [Laughter] Beautiful. I prefer real topics. What is that real thing that is showing up for you today?

Client: This is something I've been struggling with, particularly over the last couple of weeks. My dad is at end-stage cancer and is about to pass away, and this is probably one of the two most difficult relationships in my life. I have been supporting my son, who's really upset about this. I think the best way to describe the rest of my family is that they're in denial. What I'm trying to figure out for myself right now is how do I find a sense of closure before he goes? Two weeks ago, he went into the hospital with congestive heart failure, and my son right away wanted to see him. I was consumed with COVID. and wondering if that was safe. And he has school, so I felt intense resistance for myself in going. Since then, I know that I'm not going to get closure on the relationship, so I'm wondering what I could do to help myself?

Coach: I heard you use the word frozen. What would have shifted for you from being frozen to having closure for yourself at the end?

Client: Satisfied?

Coach: Okay.

Client: Or at least . . . no, that's not it. Maybe peaceful.

Coach: Is this what would be useful to explore in the short amount of time that we have to-gether? This move from frozen to peaceful in fifteen minutes?

Client: Yes. Go! [Laughter]

At this moment, the client is inviting humor into the conversation. In what is ostensibly a very delicate conversation comes a moment of levity brought by the client. We are both allowed to laugh. We do laugh. The heaviness of the issue begins to lighten, and it feels like there may be a way forward as a result.

Coach: [Laughter] Well then, let me just ask you, what does it take to begin the thawing process toward peaceful?

Client: I feel like I've worked through the negative impact this person has had on my life, so it's not about that. I could say a lot of things to him at the end, but he wouldn't be able to respond. When I was in my twenties, I used to imagine his death and how angry I would be and what I would say. But I've moved past that now. It's just that those feelings are coming up again, and I remember that fantasy from my younger self. It feels like I need to cleave that relationship, even though it sounds horrible. I've spent thirty years doing that in different ways, but it's still a struggle. The things he taught me about my-self are not who I am, but it's hard to remember that.

Holy cow! I thought this would be an easy topic, Lyssa [laughter].

Coach: You know what? It's such an important topic, and it makes me really curious about the idea of what peaceful means to you in this context. What would it take for you to have that sense of peacefulness in this topic?

Client: Actually, that's a really good question. Not even thinking about that visualization that I had when I was twenty because I've had so much guilt over the last two weeks that's come back, and I thought I had healed the anger. And it makes me really sad that I haven't completely.

           And so, shit, I'm crying with twenty-five of my closest friends [crying and laughing].

Again, the client brings forward humor as a way to release the emotion, as a way to lighten herself, and I as, the coach, join her; this is how humor can support partnership. It is crucial to the process that she feels safe and supported. Her humor is a sign that she is working to keep her mind open and creative. It is a release valve. Plus, I genuinely thought it was hilarious, her tone and words, and so we again laughed. This is what building trust sounds like: laughter and crying. The access to the humor washes away concerns about judgment, and it invites more exploration.

As the coaching conversation continues, we discuss the client's relationship with her father and how it's affecting her ability to be peaceful. The client realizes that focusing on her son, who wants to visit her father, is a more peaceful approach than dwelling on her past experiences with her parent. She also recognizes that focusing on herself is causing her to freeze and steal energy from other things. The client determines that the best way forward is to hold the focus on her son and let go of the past so that she can shine a spotlight on him and not see anything else in the shadows. Overall, the conversation helps the client find a more peaceful way of being in her father's presence.

Coach: How do you do that? How do you just shine the spot-
           light on Alex and let everything else kind of go out of
           focus?

Client: Yeah.

Coach: How do you adjust the lens to do that?

Client: Well, I think part of the way is continuing to talk to
           Alex. He and I have a tight connection anyway, so
           that's pretty easy. I think my hard part is drowning out
           the voices of the rest of the family, right? And just hear-
           ing him. I think what I probably need to do is really
           keep that dialogue going. And when I start to feel like
           I'm overfocused on feeling guilty about the anger I still
           hold and things like that, I know that I need to just talk
           to Alex and see where and how he is.

Coach: There was something you said about drowning out the
           voices of the family. I'm wondering, is there a way to
           turn down whether it's the family or your own internal
           narrative? Is there a way to turn that down so that you
           can turn up Alex?

Client: Dear God, I wish I knew [laughter]. I don't know. I
           really don't know.

Again, the humor appears, driven by the client, and as the
coach, I too can relate to her last statement. And again, we laugh and
sit with this for a bit.

We continue to discuss the client's coping strategy of disen-
gaging to deal with overwhelming situations. The client realizes that
she wants to stay engaged for her son but also detach from her own
guilt and difficult relationships with her parents. She remembers the
concept of detached involvement and sees a path forward by focusing
on her child's needs and by using her past experiences to guide her.
The conversation helps the client find a way to approach challenging
relationships while still honoring and supporting her family.

Coach: How might that support your capacity for peacefulness, turning it down?

Client: Well, I actually do see a path that way. A lot of self-care dialogue with my child and then figuring out how to be in the space not only with my dad but also with my mom and sort of go through this with a focus on what Alex is needing, and my healing, whatever it will be, will come as a by-product. Actually, that's how I've conducted my relationship with my parents for thirty years now, so I do have a model for how to do that [laughter].

Coach: [Laughter] Woot woot.

Client: Not so different.

Coach: Yeah.

Client: So it's not so different from what I already do.

Coach: What are you taking away? I'm looking at the time, and I want to be conscious of the time.

Client: Fifteen minutes.

Coach: Yeah. What are the key elements of awareness you want to hold on to from our conversation?

Client: My closure will come as a by-product of just being with these challenging relation-ships in the way I have learned to adapt to them while also honoring and supporting my son and daughter.

There was a shift as the client shared this, the lightening of energy in the conversation.

Coach: Yeah. Look at that breath and the smile.

Client: See, I knew with you it would be an easy topic [laughter].

Coach: [Laughter] There you go. What are you going to take
           away, Melanie, as far as how will you do that? Detached
           involvement. Is there anything you need to pay atten-
           tion to as you move forward?

Client: I do think this little walnut thing in my chest has been
           really tough. I have not been able to breathe for a cou-
           ple of weeks, at least since he went in the ER. And wow,
           I've got a lot more awareness of that right now because
           it's kind of relaxed. So I think that is kind of my ther-
           mometer for where is my focus and how I bring more
           self-awareness to what I'm experiencing as a mecha-
           nism for understanding what I'm focusing on as this
           whole situation continues to evolve. I think that's what
           it is.

Coach: Is there some strength or quality that you have that
           would support you in that awareness of the walnut
           when it shows up so that you have the capacity to shift
           your attention?

Client: Is that a yes/no question [laughter]?

Coach: [Laughter] I would hope that you would take it further
           than yes. But that would be leading [laughter].

Client: I don't know. A strength that I have? I don't know. I
           mean, just being self-aware. I think that's a strength,
           but it's just a thing, really.

Coach: I think it's a pretty important thing, but yeah, that
           self-awareness piece. May I offer an observation?

Client: Please.

Coach: I think it's courage that you're demonstrating, just even
           having this conversation in front of twenty-five of your
           closest friends.

Client: Yeah. I would say that my openness is probably a strength. So I could stay open to what Alex needs.

Coach: Yeah. How does that sit with you?

Client: That's good.

Coach: Is there anything else you need to claim for yourself as we bring this conversation to a bit of a con-clusion for now?

Client: I think I'm kind of proud. I mean, even though this is such a painful, painful relationship, I'm kind of proud that even at the end, I can let go of a need to express my anger at him. And I can focus on Alex, who matters to me. So I'm kind of proud of that, I think.

Coach: I'm impressed as hell.

Client: Thanks.

Coach: Does this feel like an okay place to stop?

Client: Yeah, this is good.

This conversation is another illustration of the power of met-aphors to hold the space, to move from frozen to peaceful, but also the power of letting the humor emerge and create more space for the client to do the deep work, to get to where she wants to be. The presence of humor in our conversation was instrumental; without it, it's uncertain whether we would have delved into discussions about her father or her feelings of guilt. Humor helped navigate the con-versation safely to the important underlying issue of her relationship with her child. By addressing tough issues metaphorically as frozen, hard little "walnuts" and discussing the concept of peacefulness, we were able to make a painful relationship and challenging topic more approachable and less intimidating to examine.

Wiggle Room

In this example, the topic of giving yourself grace and not being so hard on yourself is explored through the visual language of wiggle room. Maybe it's me, but the word *wiggle* is hard to take in a negative way. I think of happy puppies or little kids dancing. So when the client comes into the coaching session, the coach is at a choice point the moment the metaphor shows up.

Client: You know, I just don't want to be disappointed when I come to the end of my life. And I think, "Who am I letting down?" But it's really just me that I'm letting down. The other people in my life, like my husband, would give me a lot more wiggle room and grace than I'm giving myself.

Coach: Is giving yourself wiggle room and grace important to explore today?

Client: Yes. There's been a lot of progress in other areas of my life, I'd have to say that. Still, giving myself a little more grace and wiggle room is probably still a place I need to focus.

Coach: What do wiggle room and grace mean to you?

Client: It means I am not as hard on myself. That I give myself grace to be imperfect. And that while I hold a high standard, I also have some space to wiggle through.

Coach: If you were giving yourself more wiggle room and grace by the end of our conversation, what would that look like?

We can explore going down the road of being disappointed in one's life or what it would take to not be disappointed in one's life, which, if I am being honest, sounds heavy and negative. Or we can invite the exploration of what gives us the space to give wiggle room and grace. Which would you prefer to spend time with?

The coach tests the words, leaving the meaning of wiggle room and grace entirely open for the client to interpret in a way that fits them. We know wiggle room and grace are important, so this becomes an important place to explore. The coach can sit in the not knowing because the client clearly has a sense of knowing. So the coach can sit back, be curious, and let the client do the work.

Using the following example, we can see the competencies in the one question the coach brings forward. The client is doing the work. The coach holds the space of curiosity, listening to the client's words and their idea containers. The coach has an opportunity to support the client to explore deeper insights, all while having some linguistic fun.

Client: It's like, "Just get the certification, stop overthinking it." Telling myself, "You're going to be fine. You've invested a lot of time and money in this. It's what you really want to do in the long run." I get worried I'm wasting money. I've got some other distractions right now too, but all of this is contributing to something really important. I don't want to lose sight of my long game. Getting this done will make me proud of myself. So even as I say that, I feel like my breath quickened. It's a positive. It's like the fire in the belly thing.

Coach: What does this quickening breath and fire in the belly tell you about the importance of you sticking to your long game?

This is an example of the coach listening to the client and then using metaphors to leverage a question that invites the client to continue exploring themselves and their situation. The coach references the world that the client is creating in their mind as they speak. The client's brain lit up to the "long game" and the "fire in the belly," and their body lit up to "breath quickened," so the coach uses the words and somatic response to continue to evoke awareness with the client.

A choice point that might not be as useful is exploring what it means to waste money or whatever the fears are that are activated by the need to reassure oneself. These choices aren't wrong, as the client has shared these things, yet they don't point the way to exploring with lightness or moving forward. I also have found that if I am going to explore wasted money or a fear of some sort, I want to do that in the framework of what they want to move towards. Example: I heard you say wasted money; what is important about that in keeping your long game in sight? For most people, money is a survival topic, and it can get heavy and overwhelming quickly. In this case, the metaphors will playfully guide the conversation in a more useful direction.

I have heard many coaches explore with a leading agenda: What does it mean to waste money if you are educating yourself? In hopes the client will see how they aren't wasting money. Yet again, this isn't the important underlying issue; wasting money is a by-product of a mindset. Exploring the mindset with a forward focus—that is, the long game and what brings the fire in the belly—is a way that the client can notice and name where they want to go and then begin to consider how to support those mindsets to help them move through the discomfort of not having a crystal ball.

A Quick Reminder of Positive Emotional Attractors

The research in Chapter 5 by Boyatzis and Jack from Case Western Reserve University (2010) focused on the concept of positive emotional attractors (PEAs). Remember that PEAs help activate neural networks in the brain associated with creativity, cognitive flexibility, and learning. They sought to understand how these emotions can be leveraged in coaching and leadership development.

Through their research, Boyatzis and Jack found that coaching interactions that elicited positive emotions such as curiosity, excitement, and inspiration were more effective in promoting learning and development than interactions that were negative or neutral in tone. They also found that the use of PEAs led to more sustained behavior change over time.

I hope the key takeaway from this chapter is that playfulness and lightness are essential in supporting us to develop a range of skills necessary for life. Metaphors offer us a positive window into our own visual narrative, and a thoughtful partner can leverage our expressions to invite us to explore, open up, and navigate challenges in a playful way. Whether we're navigating social interactions, solving complex problems, or expressing our creativity, injecting playfulness offers a safe space for us to practice and refine these abilities. It's not just about having fun; it's a critical part of our development and well-being.

In restating this work, it's a reminder that the power of play, humor, and lightness open the coaching space to more creativity, flexibility, and inspirational aha moments on the part of the client, which is often the jam for most coaches.

Questions

- How does incorporating humor and playfulness into coaching sessions benefit clients in exploring and developing creative solutions?

- What will you take away about how metaphors and humor create a safe and open space for clients to delve into emotionally charged topics and find new perspectives?

- What metaphor shows up for you around bringing more playfulness into your life?

- How could you invite more play into your coaching?

Recommended Reading

Humor, Seriously: Why Humor Is a Secret Weapon in Business and Life (And How Anyone Can Harness It. Even You.) by Jennifer Aaker and Naomi Bagdonas

Chapter 16: What is Required?

" Almost everything will work again if you unplug it for a few minutes, including you.

—Anne Lamott

If we use the metaphor that you are the tool, then you are using yourself, your insights, your knowledge, and your capacity to listen deeply, ask useful questions, and hold the space for your clients. When it comes to using the metaphors your clients bring forward in a powerful way, what's required is a willingness to tune your ear to what you are listening for when your clients speak. It's simple but not easy.

Instead of the client needing you to help them examine the pros and cons of this or that, walking them through a decision tree, or giving them a worksheet as homework, the coach might listen for the metaphor of overwhelm and instead focus on the full plate, spinning discs, or juggling fire that the client is experiencing as if it is happening. I have had clients say, "I thought we were going to talk about all the stuff I am doing wrong, and I didn't want to talk about failing," and "I don't want to talk about everything I am doing wrong."

That is how clients often come to coaching—not wanting to talk about the hard stuff and afraid that it will turn into a big negative conversation about everything that isn't working.

SUPERVision

It's important for me to highlight the concept of coaching SUPERVision. Let me clarify the term, as I am spelling it with the emphasis on *SUPER* for a reason.

Unlike in clinical supervision, where a clinical supervisor participates with a supervisee to ensure the quality of clinical care, coaching SUPERVision is about collaborating with a SUPERVision partner to delve into your professional work, its impact on you, how you hold space for your clients, exploring your relationship to your work with the clients you enjoy and also those you don't enjoy, and then finding a path to creatively navigate how to hold space with your clients and take care of yourself. It's about gaining super vision—a fresh perspective, seeing things with new eyes and from different viewpoints. I believe that anyone who works with other human beings needs a place to get curious with themselves about how they are showing up.

What can happen in powerful SUPERVision is that the therapist or coach explores not only their client case but also their relationship to the case. How are we showing up? What do we do when our issues appear with our clients' issues? How do we stay patient and clear with the clients who seem to circle the drain or those we don't enjoy working with? What causes us to get hooked into teaching, telling-advice monsters? Where are we taking on too much responsibility for client outcomes and unintentionally slowing down client agency and self-awareness? These are all really important inquiries; just like our clients, we also need to do our own work.

I have been in supervision in some form or another since 1992. I believe that when working with the complexities of self and others, it's imperative to keep ourselves emotionally and mentally fit for service. Since moving to coaching from therapy, I now explore my work through the lens of coaching SUPERVision.

Early in 2023, I had a conversation with my SUPERVision partner. I was in the middle of writing this book, creating the ICF Exam PREP program, building a new learning platform for the

PREP, my mentor coaching and Power of Metaphor courses, plus remodeling my house. I felt overwhelmed. I had been talking to him about joining a SUPERVision group he was starting, but through a series of kerfuffles, I missed that meeting, and we ended up speaking one-on-one about my needs. It was clear I required support because just the sound of his voice and the overwhelm I was experiencing had me bursting into tears and crying, "I am just so overwhelmed."

He said, "I think you might be in need of restorative SUPERVision." Through my tears, I started to breathe and said, "If that's a thing, it is a thing I think I need."

We started the next week by talking about some old themes or patterns that had appeared that had me trying to do everything on my own. I was putting a lot of should's on myself that were not helping. I want to be clear: I know this stuff, and still, it's easy to default to old patterns and habits when stressed. As we talked, the idea of fit for service became a fundamental inquiry. Metaphorically, I know, I must put the oxygen on myself before helping others, but the practicality of doing that can sometimes get lost in the hurry to accomplish our work.

I was interviewing Ebony Smith, MCC, for my podcast, and she said something that has become a reminder of the importance for me: "We can't read our own label." I too need someone to help me read my label; it's hard to see it from inside the jar.

This idea clearly reminds me that I also need coaching or coaching SUPERVision. It's a reminder for all coaches to do their work; we need to have the capacity to be fit for service. Each one of us requires the support of others to be able to do the work we need to do so that we can bring our gifts to the world and be fully present, be compassionate and kind, be available to our clients and family, and hold the space for the important conversations that need to be had.

Consider that it is very difficult to hold the space for someone else when wrestling with our fears and insecurities. How do we hear the metaphors for wrestling with fear if it triggers a sense of danger inside us? How do we show up balanced and curious instead of ignoring the fear, swinging the pendulum wildly to the other side, and being overly caring or directive about what people need to do to eliminate their fear?

And, like most things, there is no "away" for emotions and our deeper drivers. There is either awareness or lack of awareness. We either work through our baggage or drag it around until we are ready to open the bags, go through all the stuff we are carrying, and Marie Kondo the crap out of it. What sparks joy? We need to do this first so that we can have empathy for the real struggle of others, digging through their crap with us.

The Ethics of Self-Care

In the world of professional support, we dedicate considerable time, compassion, and energy to those we serve. I'm deeply cognizant of the ethical obligations inherent in such roles. It's a frequent reminder of the profound need to create a supportive environment for individuals to delve into deeper introspection. While the concept of holding space may appear simple, it demands energy and emotional capacity to be fully present with whatever arises—each story, possibility, and moment of vulnerability.

From both personal experience and shared insights from peers, I recognize a crucial ethical duty: self-care. Self-care is not just a buzzword or a trendy concept; it's an essential element of ethical coaching practice.

To be truly effective, we must avoid burnout and exhaustion. You cannot be effective in your work if you are burned out, exhausted, and neglecting your own needs. When you neglect your own well-being, you run the risk of compromising the quality of care you provide to your clients.

Furthermore, the well-being of your clients is closely tied to your own well-being. You are not a robot who can simply turn your emotions or your energy on or off and leave your personal life outside of your work. Our own mental and emotional health affects our ability to empathize with our clients and provide the level of care they need.

Self-care varies greatly from person to person. For me, it involves dedicating time to my personal hobbies; establishing clear limits with myself, my clients, and my coworkers; and regularly engaging with my own coach or coaching SUPERVision partner for professional support. For others, it may mean journaling, reading a book, getting enough sleep, eating well, and engaging in physical exercise.

It's critical to understand that practicing self-care isn't an act of selfishness but an ethical imperative, particularly for coaches and those in people-focused professions. Proper self-care equips us to be at our best. The more we make it a priority, the less stress we carry, enhancing our capacity for patience, empathy, and effectiveness in our roles.

Having witnessed the detrimental impact of self-care neglect on both my personal and my professional life, I've resolved to prioritize my self-care needs. This commitment demands deliberate, daily decisions to avoid burnout, which can inadvertently harm not only us but also our clients and our businesses.

Compassionate Detachment

Compassionate detachment is a mindset or approach to dealing with difficult situations or people that lets you maintain a sense of emotional distance while still being empathetic and understanding. It is a way of setting boundaries while still being open to the other person's experience.

Compassionate detachment is the idea that I have great compassion for the journey you are on, yet I am not here to save you. I have a level of detachment that lets me be useful in my willingness to explore below the waterline with you what is important to you to notice without my own baggage getting tangled with yours. It is a crucial skill in the helping professions.

I had someone say to me many years ago, "If you want what I have, then you need to do what I do." I absolutely disagree with this perspective. This idea that what we know, our experiences, and how much courage or luck we have is the same as yours is impossible. You may be far luckier or more courageous than I am, so why would I limit you? Or you may have experienced factors I could never imagine as you navigate forward, so why would I judge you?

A well-known story that illustrates the concept of compassionate detachment is the tale of the lotus in the mud. The story goes that a beautiful lotus flower grows in a muddy pond but remains untouched and pure instead of tainted by the muddy water. The lotus symbolizes the mind, which can remain untouched by negative emotions and suffering, just like the lotus remains untouched by the mud. I would add to this idea the reality that the lotus needs the mud to grow. The mud is the nutrient-rich soil the lotus requires. The same is true for you and for your clients. We can't grow without our mud, so we might as well get into it and have a look at it.

In Buddhist philosophy, this concept is called equanimity, which teaches us to keep our minds stable, composed, and balanced in the face of life's joys, sorrows, and difficulties. I like this definition of equanimity: "Evenness of mind or temper; the quality or condition of being undisturbed by elation, depression, or agitating emotion; unruffledness" (*Oxford English Dictionary* 2023). I see it as the balance that comes from accepting things as they are and not getting too caught up in our likes and dislikes. It's just mud; we can always wash it off when we are done playing in it.

Equanimity and compassionate detachment are particularly useful in situations in which you need to take care of yourself while still being there for someone else, like say, a coach with a client who is working on hard things. Compassionate detachment is a skillful way to approach difficult circumstances and help ourselves and others. It's not always easy to balance this, but with practice and intentionality, one can learn to maintain a sense of equanimity in the face of life's ups and downs.

And, in part, this is critical for all coaches, this letting go of the need to solve, fix, or know all the details of a situation. We must open our hands and take them off the wheel of teaching, advising, and telling others what they should or should not do. What they are or are not capable of. All this is ego. If you decide that coaching is your craft, regardless of your credential level—CPC, ACC, PCC, or MCC—you can show up and hold space with your clients in a masterful way. This requires you to do your own personal development work. Take care of yourself, determine how you will hold yourself with grace, and give grace to others.

Part of that grace is the willingness to set ourselves to the side so that we can be with another person on their journey. In many ways, it is an honor that someone might trust you that much. Learning to hear and connect with that other person's internal landscape is a golden moment. For me, metaphors bring in lightness as they light up the mind. They point the way forward and support both the client and the coach to navigate the deep waters that drive actions and outcomes.

What is bubbling to the surface is a metaphor.

Metaphors give the client the clarity of distance to explore what is below the waterline with safety. Spinning plates are not as scary as "I am not living my life in a way that resonates with joy." Using metaphors in coaching is a powerful tool for listening deeply and increasing the capacity of your client to safely explore and express themselves in nonthreatening, fun, and engaging ways.

Metaphors can be used to help people make sense of their experiences, identify patterns and themes, and generate new insights. By using metaphors, coaches can create a more open, curious, and receptive environment, which can help people feel more comfortable and confident sharing their thoughts and feelings. Again, metaphors may be used unconsciously but not unintentionally.

Choose Curiosity

Throughout this book, we've been unraveling the threads of curiosity. Curiosity for the underlying themes, values, and meanings that a client brings into any coaching conversation. Testing our hypothesis and not making assumptions. When in doubt about what is important to the client, ask. When in doubt about what needs to be explored between where they are and where they want to be at the end of the coaching engagement or the coaching conversation, ask. When in doubt about what they have learned about themselves, their situation, and where they want to go through the conversation, ask. And finally, when wondering what actions will support their insights and movement toward the goals that are important to them, use your curiosity, keep your hands off the worksheets, and ask.

We know that when the coach is focused on the problem or the challenge to be solved, it is easy to slip into situational and transactional types of coaching. What did you do, how did you do it, why did you do it? If you could have done something else, what might you have done instead?

All these questions about the situation create cognitive load and strain the client's brain, taking them to places that are not as useful.

And if it's true, and I believe it is, that we are leading our clients when we ask any question, then please lead people in useful directions toward insights and awareness. Let's not lead people into what is wrong or can't be undone. Instead, lead them inside themselves, into what they have learned and what it looks like to move forward. Support your clients to be curious on their own behalf by showing up demonstrating curiosity and asking questions that only they can answer. Empower them to find the answers. Let go of the mythical checklist of best coaching questions. Show up as you, the coach, fully present and intentional, coming from a place of compassionate detachment and curious wonder. Be with your clients fully in partnership for these transformational conversations that people hunger for.

Use the International Coaching Federation competencies as a framework, not to limit you but rather to support your growth toward more partnership and deep awareness as a coach.

By listening for the metaphors the client is bringing forward, you tap into the neurocircuitry of the human mind with whom you are working. You are walking in your client's internal landscape with respect. By respecting and following the language that lights up your client's brain, you, as the coach, can support your client and move them toward more clarity, self-awareness, insight and, ultimately, actions that will genuinely support long-term sustainable changes. And that's empowering for everyone.

Happy coaching!

Questions

- What role does compassionate detachment play in maintaining a balanced and empathetic approach to coaching difficult situations or challenging clients?

- How can incorporating radical curiosity and deep listening enhance the coaching experience for both the coach and the client?

- Why is self-care an essential aspect of ethical practice for coaches, and how does it impact the quality of care provided to clients?

- What have you learned about using metaphors in your coaching, and how have metaphors impacted you or your clients to gain new insights and perspectives?

Recommended Reading

Passionate Supervision, edited by Robin Shohet

Rebel Buddha: On the Road to Freedom by Dzogchen Ponlop Rinpoche

A BIG Thank You

" Piglet noticed that even though he had a Very Small Heart, it
could hold a rather large amount of Gratitude.

— A.A. Milne, *Winnie-the-Pooh*

I want to share my deep gratitude to all the coaches and clients who
have supported my work on and about metaphors. I have learned so
much from each of you; each of you transformed my work by allowing me to play with your words. Plus, so many of you are the gener-
ous people who permitted me to record and use our coaching calls to
teach others. Thank you, thank you, thank you!

I have been fortunate to encounter incredible mentors,
teachers, SUPERVision partners, and peers, all of whom have ignit-
ed insights and aided me in weaving together coaching and metaphors. I extend my gratitude to every client I have had the privilege
to work with in therapy, coaching, mentor coaching, and coaching
SUPERVision. Each of you has introduced me to new ways of being
with others, honing my listening skills, and strengthening partner-
ships. My appreciation for each of you is boundless.

It takes a village to write a book and I want to extend very
special thanks to the team at Kirkus Editing, my sincere thanks for
ensuring the structural and grammatical precision of my work.

I would like to extend my heartfelt thanks to everyone who endorsed this book. The journey of a book is incomplete without its readers, and your words have provided tremendous support and encouragement. I am deeply grateful for your contributions to this project.

I owe a debt of gratitude to all the participants and beta readers from the 'Coaching with the Power of Metaphors Certification' program. Your insistence on shifting away from the academic dryness of research papers and the sharing of your insights and ideas has not only made the book more accessible but also enhanced its practicality. Your encouragement and support were instrumental in the evolution of this book. For this, I am ever thankful for you.

To my best friend and sister, I am not sure what my life would even look like if you weren't in it. I am grateful for your friendship, laughter, your delight in being a silly goofball with me, and your support in keeping me moving along in both my writing and my business. I know it's a little like wrangling cats when you are trying to keep me focused, and I appreciate that you allow me my flights of fancy while also bringing me back down to ground so I can get things done. Big hug, Michele.

And no acknowledgment would be complete for me without saying to my cutie, when I can have the last word, "I love you more." Thank you for supporting my endeavors for over twenty-six years. And thank you for consistently being ready for lively conversations, for a willingness to listen as I externally process through my thinking, and for wanting to sip a hot chocolate as we discuss. I am so grateful that I met you all those years ago in that coffee shop, you changed the very trajectory of my life.

Deep bow to you all.

A BIG Thank You!

We are all a sun-lit moment
come from a long darkness;

what moves us always
comes from what is hidden,

what seems to be said
so suddenly,

has lived in the body
for a long, long time.

Excerpt from 'A Seeming Stillness'
by David Whyte, *Essentials*

REFERENCES

Preface

International Coaching Federation. 2019. "ICF Core Competencies." November 2019. https://coachingfederation.org/credentials-and-standards/core-competencies.

Chapter 1

Cardillo, Eileen R., Christine E. Watson, Gwenda L. Schmidt, Alexander Kranjec, and Anjan Chatterjee. 2012. "From Novel to Familiar: Tuning the Brain for Metaphors." NeuroImage 59, no. 4: 3212–21. https://doi.org/10.1016/j.neuroimage.2011.11.079.

Chettih, Selmaan, Frank H. Durgin, and Daniel J. Grodner. 2012. "Mixing Metaphors in the Cerebral Hemispheres: What Happens When Careers Collide?" Journal of Experimental Psychology: Learning, Memory, and Cognition 38, no. 2: 295–311. DOI:10.1037/a0025862.

Duque, Anna Clara Mota, Taryn Ariadna Castro Cuesta, Ailton de Souza Melo, and Igor Lima Maldonado. 2023. "Right Hemisphere and Metaphor Comprehension: A Connectionist Perspective." Neuropsychologia 187: 108618. http://doi.org/10.1016/j.neuropsychologia.2023.108618.

Feldman Barrett, Lisa. 2020. Seven and a Half Lessons about the Brain. Boston: Mariner Books.

Felleman, Daniel J., and David C. Van Essen. 1991. "Distributed Hierarchical Processing in the Primate Cerebral Cortex." Cerebral Cortex 1, no. 1: 1–47. http://doi.org/10.1093/cercor/1.1.1-a.

Grady, Cheryl L., Anthony R. McIntosh, M. Natasha Rajah, and Fergus I. M. Craik. 1998. "Neural Correlates of the Episodic Encoding of Pictures and Words." Proceedings of the National Academy of the United States of America 95, no. 5: 2703–08.

Grady, Denise. 2019. "The Vision Thing: Mainly in the Brain." Discover Magazine, November 12, 2019. www.discovermagazine. com/mind/the-vision-thing-mainly-in-the-brain.

Massachusetts Institute of Technology. 1996. "Brain Processing of Visual Information." MIT News, December 19, 1996. https://news. mit.edu/1996/visualprocessing.

Massachusetts Institute of Technology. 1997. "Research Sheds Light on Visual Processing." MIT News, January 8, 1997. https://news. mit.edu/1997/visual-0108.

Massachusetts Institute of Technology. 2014. "In the Blink of an Eye." MIT News, January 16, 2014. https://news.mit.edu/2014/ in-the-blink-of-an-eye-0116.

Minervino, Ricardo A., Alejandra Martín, L. Micaela Tavernini, and Máximo Trench. 2018. "The Understanding of Visual Metaphors by the Congenitally Blind." Frontiers in Psychology 9: 1242. DOI:10.3389/fpsyg.2018.01242.

Chapter 2

Amin, Tamer G. 2009. "Conceptual Metaphor Meets Conceptual Change." Human Development 52, no. 3: 165–97. DOI:10.1159/000213891.

Killick, Steve, Vicki Curry, and Pamela Myles. 2016. "The Mighty Metaphor: A Collection of Therapists' Favorite Metaphors and Analogies." Cognitive Behaviour Therapist 9: e37. https://doi. org/10.1017/S1754470X16000210.

Kimmel, Michael. 2020. "Why We Mix Metaphors (and Mix Them Well): Discourse Coherence, Conceptual Metaphor, and Beyond." Journal of Pragmatics 42, no. 1 (January): 97–115.

Kövecses, Zoltán. 2010. Metaphor: A Practical Introduction. Oxford University Press.

Lakoff, George. 1993. "The Contemporary Theory of Metaphor." In Metaphor and Thought, edited by Andrew Ortony, 202–51. Cambridge: Cambridge University Press.

Lakoff, George. 2014. "Mapping the Brain's Metaphor Circuitry: Metaphorical Thought in Everyday Reason." Frontiers in Human Neuroscience 8: 958. https://doi.org/10.3389/fnhum.2014.00958.

Lakoff, George, and Mark Johnson. 1980. Metaphors We Live By. Chicago: University of Chicago Press.

Liddell, Henry George, and Robert Scott. 1901. A Greek-English Lexicon. Oxford, UK: Clarendon Press.

Malkomsen, A., J. I. Røssberg, T. Dammen, T. Wilberg, A. Løvgren, R. Ulberg, and J. Evensen. 2022. "How Therapists in Cognitive Behavioral and Psychodynamic Therapy Reflect upon the Use of Metaphors in Therapy: A Qualitative Study." BMC Psychiatry 22, no. 1: 1–12.

Mathieson, Fiona, Jennifer Jordan, Janet D. Carter, and Maria Stubbe. 2016. "Nailing Down Metaphors in CBT: Definition, Identification and Frequency." Behavioural and Cognitive Psychotherapy 44, no. 2 (March): 236–48.

Pollio, Howard R., Jack M. Barlow, Harold J. Fine, and Marilyn R. Pollio. 1977. Psychology and the Poetics of Growth: Figurative Language in Psychology, Psychotherapy, and Education. Hillsdale, NJ: Erlbaum.

Reddy, Michael J. 1979. The Conduit Metaphor: A Case of Frame Conflict in Our Language about Language. Cambridge: Cambridge University Press.

Siegelman, Ellen Y. 1990. Metaphor and Meaning in Psychotherapy. New York: Guilford Press.

Stott, Richard, Warren Mansell, Paul Salkovskis, Anna Lavender, and Sam Cartwright-Hatton. 2010. Oxford Guide to Metaphors in CBT: Building Cognitive Bridges. Oxford, UK: Oxford University Press.

Tosey, Paul, Wendy Sullivan, and Margaret Meyer. 2013. Clean Sources: Six Metaphors a Minute? England: University of Surrey.

Wickman, Scott Allen, Harry M. Daniels, Lyle J. White, and

Steven A. Fesmire. 1999. "A 'Primer' in Conceptual Metaphor for Counselors." Journal of Counseling and Development 77, no. 4: 389–94. https://doii.org/10.1002/j.1556-6676.1999.tb02464.x.

Chapter 3

Baron-Cohen, Simon, Sally Wheelwright, Jacqueline Hill, Yogini Raste, and Ian Plumb. 2001. "The 'Reading the Mind in the Eyes' Test Revised Version: A Study with Normal Adults, and Adults with Asperger Syndrome or High-Functioning Autism." Journal of Child Psychology and Psychiatry 42, no. 2: 241–51.

Chen, Hui, and Brad Wyble. 2016. "Attribute Amnesia Reflects a Lack of Memory Consolidation for Attended Information." Journal of Experimental Psychology: Human Perception and Performance 42, no. 2: 225–34. DOI:10.1037/xhp0000133.

Fearne, Michael. 2020. The LSP Method: How to Engage People and Spark Insights Using the LEGO® Serious Play® Method. Austin, TX: Lioncrest.

Prutting, Carol A., and Diane M. Kirchner. 1987. "Metaphor Comprehension in Aphasia." Brain and Language 31, no. 1: 91–116.

Chapter 4

Panayotov, Plamen, and Boyan Strahilov, eds. 2019. Signs on the Road from Therapy to Conversations Led by Clients. London: Lambert Academic Publishing.

Rogers, Carl R. 1942. Counseling and Psychotherapy: Newer Concepts in Practice. Boston: Houghton Mifflin.

Rogers, Carl R., Harold C. Lyon Jr., and Reinhard Tausch. 2013. On Becoming an Effective Teacher: Person-Centered Teaching, Psychology, Philosophy, and Dialogues with Carl R. Rogers and Harold Lyon. London: Routledge.

Siminovitch, Dorothy E. 2022. A Gestalt Coaching Primer: The Path toward Awareness Intelligence. 2nd ed. Toronto: Gestalt Coaching Works.

Chapter 5

Boyatzis, Richard E., and Anthony I. Jack. 2018. "The Neuroscience of Coaching." Consulting Psychology Journal: Practice and Research 70, no. 1: 11–27. https://doi.org./10.1037/cpb0000095.

Boyatzis, Richard E., Kylie Rochford, and Scott N. Taylor. 2015. "The Role of the Positive Emotional Attractor in Vision and Shared Vision: Toward Effective Leadership, Relationships, and Engagement." Frontiers in Psychology 6: 670. http://doi:10.3389/fpsyg.2015.00670.

Bradshaw, John. 1988. Healing the Shame That Binds You. Deerfield Beach, FL: Health Communications.

Brown, Brené. 2015. Daring Greatly: How the Courage to Be Vulnerable Transforms the Way We Live, Love, Parent, and Lead. New York: Avery.

Case Western Reserve University. 2010. "Coaching with Compassion Can 'Light Up' Human Thoughts." ScienceDaily, November 19, 2010. www.sciencedaily.com/releases/2010/11/101117184501.htm.

Jack, Anthony I., Richard E. Boyatzis, Masud S. Khawaja, Angela M. Passarelli, and Regina L. Leckie. 2013. "Visioning in the Brain: An fMRI Study of Inspirational Coaching and Mentoring." Social Neuroscience 8, no. 4: 369–84. https://doi.org/10.1080/17470919.2013.808259.

Panayotov, Plamen, and Boyan Strahilov, eds. 2019. Signs on the Road from Therapy to Conversations Led by Clients. London: Lambert Academic Publishing.

Chapter 6

Clark, Ruth C., Frank Nguyen, and John Sweller. 2006. Efficiency in Learning: Evidence-Based Guidelines to Manage Cognitive Load. Hoboken, NJ: Wiley.

Lakoff, George, and Mark Johnson. 1980. Metaphors We Live By. Chicago: University of Chicago Press.

Marschark, Marc, and R. Reed Hunt. 1989. "The Additive Effects of Semantically Related and Unrelated Words and Pictures on Memory: Implications for Dual Coding Theory." Journal of Experimental Psychology: Learning, Memory, and Cognition 15, no. 2: 179.

Paivio, Allan. 1986. Mental Representations: A Dual Coding Approach. Oxford, UK: Oxford University Press.

Paivio, Allan, and James M. Clark. 1991. "Dual Coding Theory and Education." Educational Psychology Review 3, no. 3: 149–210.

Plass, Jan L., Roxana Moreno, and Roland Brünken, eds. 2010. Cognitive Load Theory. Cambridge: Cambridge University Press.

Sweller, John. 1988. "Cognitive Load during Problem Solving: Effects on Learning." Cognitive Science 12, no. 2 (April): 257–85.

Willingham, Daniel T. 2009. Why Don't Students Like School? A Cognitive Scientist Answers Questions about How the Mind Works and What It Means for the Classroom. San Francisco: Jossey-Bass.

Chapter 7

Lawley, James. 2023. "Context Makes Clean Clean." CleanLanguage.com. August 2023. https://cleanlanguage.com/context-makes-clean-clean.

Sullivan, Wendy, and Judy Rees. 2008. Clean Language: Revealing Metaphors and Opening Minds. Bethel, CT: Crown House.

Tompkins, Penny, and James Lawley. 1997. "Less Is More . . . The Art of Clean Language." Rapport 35 (February).

Tompkins, Penny, Wendy Sullivan, and James Lawley. 2005. "Tangled Spaghetti in My Head." CleanLanguage.com. October 2005. https://cleanlanguage.com/tangled-spaghetti-in-my-head.

Chapter 8

Armour, J. Andrew. 1991. "Intrinsic Cardiac Neurons." Journal of Cardiovascular Electrophysiology 2, no. 4 (August): 331–341. https://doi.org/10.1111/j.1540-8167.1991.tb01330.x.

References

Childre, Doc, and Howard Martin. 2000. The HeartMath Solution: The Institute of HeartMath's Revolutionary Program for Engaging the Power of the Heart's Intelligence. New York: HarperCollins.

Desai, Rutvik H. 2021. "Are Metaphors Embodied? The Neural Evidence." Psychological Research 86: 2417–33. https://doi.org/10.1007/s00426-021-01604-4.

HeartMath Institute. 2023. "Heart Coherence." www.heartmath.org/heart-coherence.

Herculano-Houzel, Suzana. 2009. "The Human Brain in Numbers: A Linearly Scaled-Up Primate Brain." Frontiers in Human Neuroscience 3 (November): 31. https://doi.org/10.3389/neuro.09.031.2009.

Kandasamy, Narayanan, Sarah N. Garfinkel, Lionel Page, Ben Hardy, Hugo D. Critchley, Mark Gurnell, and John M. Coates. 2016. "Interoceptive Ability Predicts Survival on a London Trading Floor." Scientific Reports 6: 32986. https://doi.org/10.1038/srep32986.

Kandel, Eric R., James H. Schwartz, Thomas M. Jessell, Steven A. Siegelbaum, and A. J. Hudspeth, eds. 2013. Principles of Neural Science. 5th ed. New York: McGraw-Hill.

Mayer, Emeran A. 2011. "Gut Feelings: The Emerging Biology of Gut–Brain Communication." Nature Reviews Neuroscience 12, no. 8: 453–66. http://doi.org/10.1038/nrn3071.

Porges, Stephen W. 2011. The Polyvagal Theory: Neurophysiological Foundations of Emotions, Attachment, Communication, and Self-Regulation. New York: W. W. Norton.

van der Kolk, Bessel. 2015. The Body Keeps the Score: Brain, Mind, and Body in the Healing of Trauma. New York: Penguin.

Varela, Francisco J., Evan Thompson, and Eleanor Rosch. 2016. The Embodied Mind: Cognitive Science and Human Experience. Cambridge, MA: MIT Press.

Verny, Thomas R. 2021. The Embodied Mind: Understanding the

Mysteries of Cellular Memory, Consciousness, and Our Bodies. New York: Pegasus Books.

Wilson, Margaret. 2008. "How Did We Get from There to Here? An Evolutionary Perspective on Embodied Cognition." In Perspectives on Cognitive Science, 373–93. https://doi.org/10.1016/B978-0-08-046616-3.00019-0.

Chapter 9

Alshami, Ali M. 2019. "Pain: Is It All in the Brain or the Heart?" Current Pain and Headache Reports 23, no. 12: 88. DOI:10.1007/s11916-019-0827-4.

Armour, J. Andrew. 1991. "Intrinsic Cardiac Neurons." Journal of Cardiovascular Electrophysiology 2, no. 4 (August): 331–41. https://doi.org/10.1111/j.1540-8167.1991.tb01330.x.

Childre, Doc, and Howard Martin. 2000. The HeartMath Solution: The Institute of HeartMath's Revolutionary Program for Engaging the Power of the Heart's Intelligence. New York: HarperCollins.

Eastman, Quinn. 2012. "Metaphors Activate Sensory Areas of Brain." Woodruff Health Sciences Center. https://news.emory.edu/stories/2012/02/metaphor_brain_imaging/

HeartMath Institute. 2023. "Heart Coherence." www.heartmath.org/heart-coherence.

Miller, Michael. 2019. "Emotional Rescue: The Heart-Brain Connection." Cerebrum (May–June).

Silsbee, Doug. 2008. Presence-Based Coaching: Cultivating Self-Generative Leaders through Mind, Body, and Heart. San Francisco: Jossey-Bass.

Soosalu, Grant, and Marvin Oka. 2012. mBraining: Using Your Multiple Brains to Do Cool Stuff. Seattle: CreateSpace.

Chapter 10

International Coaching Federation. 2020a. "ICF Code of Ethics." January 2020. https://coachingfederation.org/ethics/code-of-ethics.

International Coaching Federation. 2020b. "Professional Certified Coach (PCC) Markers." November 2020. https://coachfederation.org/app/uploads/2020/11/Updated-PCC-Markers_November-2020.pdf.

Chapter 11

International Coaching Federation. 2020. "ICF Core Competencies." January 2020. https://coachingfederation.org/ethics/code-of-ethics.

Chapter 12

Frankl, Viktor E. 1988. Man's Search for Meaning. New York: Washington Square Press.

Jackson, Kitty. 2017. "Symbolism in Art: The Egg." ArtDependence Magazine, June 5, 2017. www.artdependence.com/articles/symbolism-in-art-the-egg.

Chapter 13

Feldman Barrett, Lisa. 2020. Seven and a Half Lessons about the Brain. Boston: Mariner Books.

deHart, Lyssa Danehy. 2017. StoryJacking: Change Your Inner Dialogue, Transform Your Life. New York: Aviva.

Chapter 14

Bright, Neil. 2018. Rethinking Everything: Personal Growth through Transactional Analysis. 2nd ed. Lanham, MD: Rowman & Littlefield.

Carpenter, Siri. 2008. "Buried Prejudice: The Bigot in Your Brain." Scientific American 19, no. 2, 32–39. https://doi.org/10.1038/scientificamericanmind0408-32.

Edmondson, Amy C. 2018. The Fearless Organization: Creating Psychological Safety in the Workplace for Learning, Innovation, and Growth. Hoboken, NJ: Wiley.

Harris, Thomas. 2004. I'm OK—You're OK. New York: Harper

Perennial.

Zaldivar, Enrique J. 2020. Your Unique Cultural Lens: A Guide to Cultural Competence. Hinsdale, MA: Inspired Inc.

Chapter 15

Aaker, Jennifer, and Naomi Bagdonas. 2020. Humor, Seriously: Why Humor Is a Secret Weapon in Business and Life (And How Anyone Can Harness It. Even You.) New York: Random House.

American Physiological Society. 2008. "Anticipating a Laugh Reduces Our Stress Hormones, Study Shows." ScienceDaily, April 10, 2008. www.sciencedaily.com/releases/2008/04/080407114617. htm.

Arnsten, Amy, Carolyn M. Mazure, and Rajita Sinha. 2012. "This Is Your Brain in Meltdown." Scientific American 306, no. 4: 48–53. https://doi.org/10.1038/scientificamerican0412-48.

Brown, Stuart, and Christopher Vaughan. 2009. Play: How It Shapes the Brain, Opens the Imagination, and Invigorates the Soul. New York: Avery.

Cannon, Walter B. 1963. The Wisdom of the Body. New York: W. W. Norton.

Case Western Reserve University. 2010. "Coaching with Compassion Can 'Light Up' Human Thoughts." ScienceDaily, November 19, 2010. www.sciencedaily.com/releas-es/2010/11/101117184501.htm.

Robinson, Lawrence, Melinda Smith, and Jeanne Segal. 2023. "Laughter Is the Best Medicine." HelpGuide.Org, February 28, 2023. www.helpguide.org/articles/mental-health/laughter-is-the-best-medicine.htm.

Wang, Mengke, and Zengzhao, Chen. 2022. "Laugh before You Study: Does Watching Funny Videos before Study Facilitate Learning?" International Journal of Environmental Research and Public Health 19, no. 8: 4434. https://doi.org/10.3390/ijerph19084434.

Chapter 16

Oxford English Dictionary. s.v. "Equanimity, (n.)."
Accessed November 25, 2023. www.oed.com/search/
dictionary/?scope=Entries&q=equanimity.

ABOUT LYSSA

Hello, I'm Lyssa deHart. I spent twenty years as a clinical social worker specializing in relationship therapy, complex trauma, PTSD, and dissociative disorders. After closing my private practice in New Mexico and relocating to the Pacific Northwest in 2013, I fully embraced coaching.

I achieved my MCC certification in 2018 and have been dedicated to this path ever since. I am the host the Coaching Studio podcast and am a leadership and confidence coach, certified mentor coach, coaching SUPERVision partner, ICF PCC assessor, and a well-regarded coaching educator.

I authored *StoryJacking: Change Your Dialogue, Transform Your Life* and *the Reflective Coach*. My latest work, *Light Up: The Science of Coaching with Metaphors,* reflects my deep commitment to enhancing coaching practices, emphasizing partnership, client agency, and the mastery of coaching skills.

With a solid understanding of ICF core competencies and neuroscience, I am passionate about empowering coaches and therapists to improve their listening and partnering abilities, enhance their presence, and create nurturing environments for client growth. My global practice serves clients across continents and numerous countries. I focus on helping professional coaches and therapists make a significant impact, infusing their work with ease and a sense of fun.

Additionally, I developed the Coach Credentialing Exam PREP, an essential course and toolkit for coaches facing the challenges of the ICF exam. My personal experience with dyslexia led me to create a program that helps other coaches internalize the ICF competencies and code of ethics, thereby enhancing their chances of success in taking the exam.

My work with metaphors culminated in the innovative Power of Metaphor Certification Program, aimed at sharpening coaches' listening skills and using the power of metaphors to foster strong agreements, build deep trust, unleash potential, and enhance awareness—key elements of lasting transformation. I offer this certification to both coaches and therapists. This book draws directly from the teachings of the Level 1 Certification program.

Thank you for exploring this book. I hope it provides valuable insights for your client work. I have a request: Your feedback is incredibly important; please consider sharing your thoughts with a review on Amazon.com. Your support is greatly appreciated. Just follow the QR code to leave a review :)

Let's connect:

Website: www.LyssadeHart.com

YouTube: @LyssadeHart

LinkedIn: https://www.linkedin.com/in/lyssadehart

What has been most useful and/or valuable to you as you have gone through this book?

● ●

Before you put this book away, what are a couple of skills you want to play with in your coaching? By writing them down you will be creating an intention for yourself.

_____

_____

_____

_____

_____

_____

_____

_____

_____

_____

_____

_____

Bravo and Happy Coaching!

www.ingramcontent.com/pod-product-compliance
Lightning Source LLC
Chambersburg PA
CBHW070106030426
42335CB00016B/2032